Building an IoT Node
for less than $ 15

Claus Kühnel

Building an IoT Node
for less than $ 15

NodeMCU & ESP8266

Claus Kühnel

ISBN-10: 3-907857-30-5

ISBN-13: 978-3-907857-30-4

www.ckskript.ch

The book and the circuits described, procedures and programs, have been carefully created and tested. Nevertheless, errors and mistakes cannot be excluded.

The front cover image based on Fotalia image:
File: #79214299 | Author: chombosan.

Contents

1. Preface

These days, everyone is talking about the "Internet of Things", and what the future will bring in this field. As early as 1966, Karl Steinbuch, a German computer science pioneer, said: *"In a few decades' time, computers will be interwoven into almost every industrial product."*

As shown in the IoT roadmap (Figure 1), we can see that Karl Steinbuch's vision is already a reality, with high potential for further development.

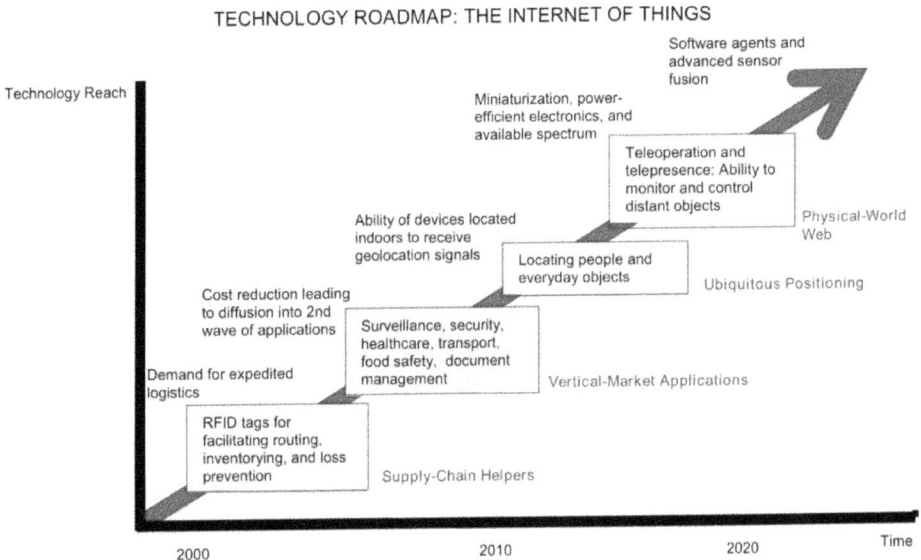

TECHNOLOGY ROADMAP: THE INTERNET OF THINGS

Software agents and advanced sensor fusion

Technology Reach

Miniaturization, power-efficient electronics, and available spectrum

Teleoperation and telepresence: Ability to monitor and control distant objects

Physical-World Web

Ability of devices located indoors to receive geolocation signals

Locating people and everyday objects

Ubiquitous Positioning

Cost reduction leading to diffusion into 2nd wave of applications

Surveillance, security, healthcare, transport, food safety, document management

Vertical-Market Applications

Demand for expedited logistics

RFID tags for facilitating routing, inventorying, and loss prevention

Supply-Chain Helpers

2000   2010   2020   Time

Source: SRI Consulting Business Intelligence

Figure 1 Technology Roadmap—The Internet of Things

A lot of explanations for the Internet of Things (IoT) can be found if one searches the web. There is a good article on Wikipedia (http://goo.gl/Y3DCLN), but I also like an article from Forbes magazine, titled "A Simple Explanation of 'The Internet Of Things'" (http://goo.gl/WQUVKM).

There, Jacob Morgan defines the IoT as follows: "Simply put, this is the concept of basically connecting any device with an on and off switch to the Internet (and/or to each other)".

This includes everything from cell phones, coffee makers, washing machines, headphones, lamps, wearable devices and almost anything else one can think of. This also applies to components of machines, for example, a jet engine of an airplane, or the drill of an oilrig. As I mentioned, if it has an on and off switch, then chances are it can be a part of the IoT.

The analyst firm Gartner says that by 2020, there would be over 26 billion connected devices...that's a lot of connections (some even estimate this number to be much higher, over 100 billion). The IoT is a giant network of connected "things" (which also includes people). The relationship will be between people and people, people and things, and things and things.

The new rule for the future is going to be: "Anything that can be connected will be connected."

In this book, we will consider the frontend of the IoT—the so-called IoT node. This IoT node is connected to sensors and actors and to the network. Our IoT node uses WLAN connectivity to the network, with which it is very easy to integrate it into an existing office or home network.

This task can be fulfilled by a lot of wireless network-capable microcontrollers, such as Arduino, Raspberry Pi, Beagle Bone and those furthermore equipped with Wi-Fi devices. But the use of such complex devices is not in focus here. Our goal is to use a very cheap device to build a compact IoT node.

The title of this book defines our goal: building an IoT Node for less than $ 15. A listing of expected costs for the various components is given in Chapter 0, listing the IoT node costs.

The ESP8266 microcontroller is the base for this journey. Let's start from there.

All listed sources and some explanations can be found at SourceForge under http://sourceforge.net/projects/nodemcu/. Furthermore, I comment on news and personal experience in the blog https://cknodemcu.wordpress.com/

For easy readability, I have followed the conventions listed below in the textual representation:

- Commands and output to the console are represented in `Courier New`.
- Inputs via console are in `Courier New`.
- Program and file names appear in *Italian*.

Long URLs will be shortened by Google's URL shortener.

All existing links were checked in the autumn of 2015. As the Internet changes continuously, it cannot be ensured that these links will work or lead to the same content as at the time of admission. Please inform me about broken links.

Altendorf, autumn 2015

Claus Kühnel

2. ESP8266 System-on-Chip

The ESP8266 System-on-Chip (SOC) offers a complete and self-contained Wi-Fi networking solution; it can be used to host the application, or offload Wi-Fi networking functions from another application processor.

When ESP8266 hosts the application, it boots up directly from an external flash. It has an integrated cache to improve the performance of the system in such applications.

Alternatively, serving as a Wi-Fi adapter, wireless Internet access can be added to any microcontroller-based design with simple connectivity (SPI/SDIO or I^{2}C/UART interface).

ESP8266 is among the most integrated Wi-Fi chips in the industry; it integrates the antenna switches, RF balun, power amplifier, low noise receiving amplifier, filters, power management modules. It requires minimal external circuitry, and the entire solution, including front-end module, is designed to occupy a minimal PCB area.

ESP8266 also integrates an enhanced version of Tensilica's L106 Diamond series 32-bit processor (http://goo.gl/1gFOYk), with on-chip SRAM, apart from the Wi-Fi functionalities. ESP8266 is often integrated with external sensors and other application-specific devices through its GPIOs; sample codes for such applications are provided in the software development kit (SDK).

The following Espressif documents describe the ESP8266 in detail:

- ES8266EX Datasheet
  http://bbs.espressif.com/download/file.php?id=394

- ESP8266EX Hardware User Guide
  http://bbs.espressif.com/download/file.php?id=405

2.1. Chip

The ESP8266EX microcontroller chip is the base for several ESP modules.

Here, only the main features are listed. Please refer to the datasheet for complete specifications of the ESP8266EX microcontroller.

- Network standards 802.11 b/g/n
- Integrated low power 32-bit MCU
- Integrated 10-bit ADC
- Integrated TCP/IP protocol stack
- Integrated PLL, regulators, and power management units
- Wi-Fi 2.4 GHz, support WPA/WPA2
- Support STA/AP/STA+AP operation modes
- SDIO 2.0, (H) SPI, UART, I2C, I2S, IR Remote Control, PWM, GPIO
- Deep sleep power < 5uA
- Wake up and transmit packets in < 2ms
- Super small module size (11.5 mm x 11.5 mm)
- Operating temperature range -40C ~ 125C
- FCC, CE, TELEC, Wi-Fi Alliance, and SRRC certified

The ESP8266EX microcontroller chip conforms to RoHS and has all required certificates, such as

FC   FCC identifier: 2AC7Z-ESP8266EX

C E   CE number: TCF-1933CC14

Therefore, no restrictions on its use in applications are expected.

Figure 2 shows some ESP8266EX chips in QFN32 packages.

Figure 2 ESP8266EX Chips

Figure 3 shows the pinout of the ESP8266EX chip.

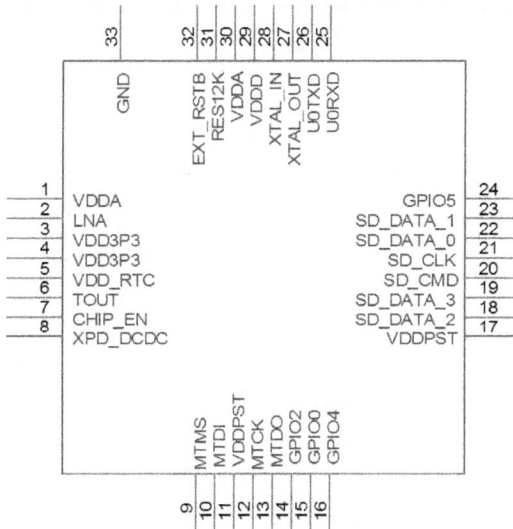

Figure 3 ESP8266EX Pinout

2.2. Modules

To build the complete working infrastructure, some external components around the ESP8266EX are required. Figure 4 shows the ESP8266EX schematic with SPI Flash U3, crystal U2 and the antenna connector ANT1.

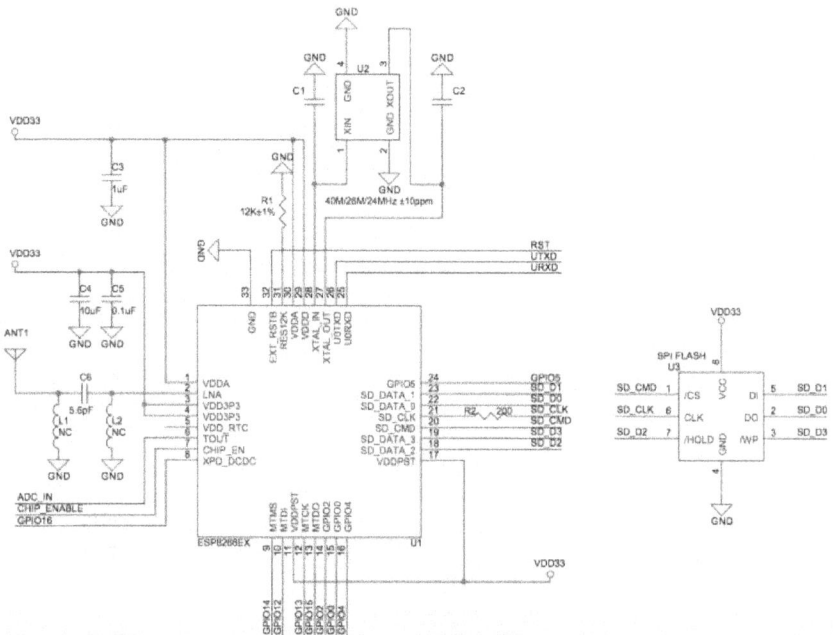

Figure 4 ESP8266EX Schematic

This infrastructure is normally assembled as an ESP8266 module, of which there are many different variants.

Table 1 shows an outline of the ESP8266 module family, as listed in ESP8266 community wiki (http://goo.gl/CgisDm).

Board ID	pins	pitch	form factor	LED	Antenna	Ant. Socket	Shield	dimensions mm
ESP-01	8	.1"	2×4 DIL	Yes	Etched-on PCB	No	No	14.3 x 24.8
ESP-02	8	.1"	2×4 notch	No?	None	Yes	No	14.2 x 14.2
ESP-03	14	2 mm	2×7 notch	No	Ceramic	No	No	17.3 x 12.1
ESP-04	14	2 mm	2×4 notch	No?	None	No	No	14.7 x 12.1
ESP-05	5	.1"	1×5 SIL	No	None	Yes	No	14.2 x 14.2
ESP-06	12+ GND	misc	4×3 dice	No	None	No	Yes	?
ESP-07	16	2 mm	2×8 pinhole	Yes	Ceramic	Yes	Yes	20.0 x 16.0
ESP-08	14	2 mm	2×7 notch	No	None	No	Yes	17.0 x 16.0
ESP-09	12+ GND	misc	4×3 dice	No	None	No	No	10.0 x 10.0
ESP-10	5	2 mm?	1×5 notch	No	None	No	No	14.2 x 10.0
ESP-11	8	1.27 mm	1×8 pinhole	No?	Ceramic	No	No	17.3 x 12.1
ESP-12	16	2 mm	2×8 notch	Yes	Etched-on PCB	No	Yes	24.0 x 16.0
ESP-12-E	22	2 mm	2×8 notch	Yes	Etched-on PCB	No	Yes	24.0 x 16.0
ESP-13	18	1.5 mm	2×9	?	Etched-on PCB	No	Yes	? x ?
WROOM-02	18	1.5 mm	2×9	No	Etched-on PCB	No	Yes	20.0 x 18.0
WT8266-S1	18	1.5 mm	3×6	1	Etched-on PCB	No	Yes	15.0 x 18.6

Table 1 ESP8266 Module Family

The ESP-12 module is widely used because it handles well. Figure 5 shows this module with a shielded ESP8266EX and the antenna etched on the right side.

Figure 5 ESP-12 module with shielded ESP8266EX and etched antenna

In the meantime, other ESP8266 modules are offered by further vendors. A small selection will be presented here (Table 2).

Module	Name	Vendor	URL
	NodeMCU LUA Amica R2	Electrodragon	http://goo.gl/M1VI0Q
	NodeMCU v2	SeeedStudio	http://goo.gl/CJLY5q
	HUZZAH ESP8266 Breakout	Adafruit	https://goo.gl/thfn8t
	SparkFun ESP8266 Thing	SparkFun	https://goo.gl/3aBukO
	ESP-ADC Module with ESP8266EX	In-Circuit	http://goo.gl/LIxT4h
	ESP8266-EVB	Olimex	https://goo.gl/uhaUK8

	Espressif WROOM-02	Espressif	http://goo.gl/paUwUP
	SparkFun Wi-Fi Shield - ESP8266	Sparkfun	https://goo.gl/w72mNt

Table 2 ESP8266 Modules

Some of the modules shown in Table 2 use an ESP-12 module on-board and serve as a base board for that. The serial interface is used as a communication interface for firmware and program download.

From Figure 4, we can see that the pins UTXD & URXD are connected directly to the ESP8266 chip. This means that we have to pay attention to the logic level. If there are no level shifters on board, then we have to connect serial lines with 3.3 V logic level.

GPIO0 of the ESP8266 device is used to activate the boot-loader for firmware update via serial interface. Connecting this pin to GND during power-up or reset will activate the boot-loader.

Some of the modules listed in Table 2 have additional components around the ESP8266 device. Peculiarities of the individual modules that have to be observed are described in the following chapters.

2.2.1. NodeMCU-devkit

The NodeMCU-devkits already have a CP2102 USB to UART bridge and a voltage regulator on board each. So, we can connect the NodeMCU-devkit with a normal USB cable to a PC for communication and power supply.

Furthermore, the module has an auto program circuit, which controls the activation of the boot-loader. No key must be pressed.

We have to consider 3.3 V logic levels only for digital IO; one will need to level shift any 5 V signals running into the NodeMCU device.

The schematic for the NodeMCU-devkit is saved at GitHub (https://goo.gl/7xkiAf) and can be downloaded from there.

The NodeMCU firmware is already installed. It is possible that newer firmware versions are available. If one wishes to use such an updated firmware, then one can re-program the module anytime.

2.2.2. Adafruit Huzzah Board

The Huzzah Board from Adafruit has only a few components around the ESP-12 module, like a voltage regulator, two keys (Reset, User), and a red LED.

The Huzzah Board must be connected with a so-called console cable to the USB interface of the PC for communication and power supply. This connection is explained in Chapter 2.3.

The digital IO operates with the 3.3 V level again, as one can see from the schematic on Adafruit's website https://goo.gl/XX9DPY.

The NodeMCU firmware is already installed. If one wishes to update it, then one would have to switch into boot-loader mode by pressing the GPIO0 key while booting (after pressing the Reset key).

2.2.3. SparkFun ESP8266 Thing

The SparkFun ESP8266 Thing is a breakout and development board for the ESP8266 device. The pins are broken out to two parallel, bread board-compatible rows. The ESP8266 Thing has a LiPo charger added; hence, it is prepared to operate as an IoT node autonomous.

The USB connector serves only as a power connector. For program download, we have to use the FTDI connector. The ESP8266's maximum voltage is 3.6V, so the ESP8266 Thing has an on-board 3.3V regulator to deliver a safe, consistent voltage to the IC. This means that the ESP8266's I/O pins also run at 3.3V; one will need to level shift any 5V signals running into the IC. The schematic of the ESP8266 Thing can be downloaded from https://goo.gl/bTkZ44.

The ESP8266 Thing is prepared for installing some I^2C devices.

Device	Manufacturer	Function	Link
ECC 108	Atmel	ECC-based Crypto Element	http://goo.gl/yvNYAu
TMP102	TI	Low-Power Digital Temperature Sensor	http://goo.gl/x51bMp
TSL2561	TAOS	Light-to-Digital Converter	http://goo.gl/xyD48h

Normally, these devices are not populated.

A 3.3V FTDI Basic is required to program the SparkFun ESP8266 Thing, but other serial converters with 3.3V I/O levels should work just fine as well. The converter does need a DTR line in addition to the RX and TX pins.

The debug interface, described in Chapter 2.3, has no DTR line. To switch the ESP8266 Thing into the boot-loader mode, we would have to connect GPIO0 to GND in the sequence already explained.

The ESP8266 Thing must be programmed with the NodeMCU firmware at first. The programming itself is done, as described in Chapter 5.1. I have the ESP8266 Thing flashed with the firmware *nodemcu_float_0.9.6_dev_20150704.bin*.

2.2.4. ESP-ADC Module

The ESP-ADC Module is designed for integration into other circuits, and contains only the necessary wiring for the ESP8266 Chip.

Powering and serial communication must, therefore, be done with 3.3 V levels. In addition, the module has to be brought into the boot-loader mode manually, by connecting GPIO0 to GND before switching on the operating voltage.

I have built the whole thing on a bread board (Figure 6). On the right side is a switchable power supply, to see that the property is set for 3.3 V DC. Below the ESP-ADC, one can see the jumpers for the power supply and the serial ports to the debug interface (described in Chapter 2.3).

Figure 6 ESP-ADC on a Bread Board

The programming itself is done, as described in Chapter 5.1. I have the ESP-ADC flashed with the firmware *nodemcu_float_0.9.6_dev_20150704.bin*.

2.2.5. Olimex ESP8266-EVB

The ESP8266-EVB is an evaluation board for the ESP8266 device that has a relay, a key and the Olimex UEXT expansion connector. All GPIOs are available at header CON3.

Figure 7 shows the pinout of this UEXT expansion connector. The schematic of the complete ESP8266-EVB can be downloaded from https://goo.gl/vykby2.

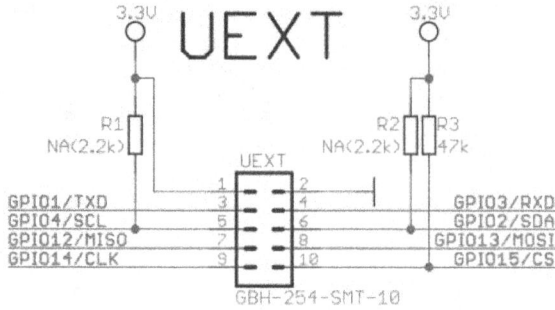

Figure 7 UEXT Expansion Connector

The power supply of the module is via a plug with 5 V DC. The serial communication must be done with 3.3 V levels. The debug interface will be connected via the UEXT expansion connector.

The module goes into boot-loader mode by pressing the key BUT in a sequence already explained.

The programming itself is done, as described in Chapter 5.1. I have the ESP8266-EVB flashed with the firmware *nodemcu_float_0.9.6_dev_20150704.bin*.

2.2.6. ESP-WROOM-02

Espressif, as the manufacturer of the ESP8266, offers the ESP-WROOM-02 as an own Wi-Fi module. It will be delivered as a module for integration.

The assembly on a breakout board helps in handling the module in an easier way. I used the breakout board offered by the Japanese company SwitchScience (https://goo.gl/XTsa8T). Figure 8 shows an ESP-WROOM-02 mounted on such a breakout board.

Figure 8 ESP-WROOM-02 mounted on a Breakout Board

After soldering the module and the headers, one can use the module on breadboard, as usual. The module must be powered with 3.3 V DC, and all IO levels are 3.3 V, too.

Therefore, the handling of this module can be compared with the ESP-ADC module.

2.2.7. Sparkfun ESP8266 Wi-Fi Shield

The SparkFun ESP8266 Wi-Fi Shield is an Arduino compatible shield for the ESP8266 device. The ESP8266 Wi-Fi Shield finds a middle ground between the ESP8266 Module and the ESP8266 Thing that provides a great introduction to the ESP8266, without having to leave the comfortable hardware confines of the Arduino. If one just has an Arduino project that needs an inexpensive gateway to the Internet, the ESP8266 Wi-Fi Shield does everything from turning on an LED to posting data with phant.io.

Nevertheless, we will use the SparkFun ESP8266 Wi-Fi Shield as an independent controller that can be connected with Arduino shields for IO expansion.

The power supply is provided by the FTDI or Arduino 5 V DC connector. A power regulator internally converts this 5 V into 3.3 V DC. The serial communication can operate with 5 V level because on-board level shifters are installed. The debug interface will be connected via FTDI pin header. The schematics can be downloaded from https://goo.gl/v1lUz1.

23

The SparkFun ESP8266 Wi-Fi Shield goes into boot-loader mode by connecting GPIO0 to GND in the sequence already explained.

The programming itself is done, as described in Chapter 5.1. I have the ESP8266-EVB flashed with the firmware *nodemcu_float_0.9.6_dev_20150704.bin*.

2.2.8. Protoneer WifiPixels

WifiPixels, manufactured by Protoneer from New Zealand, are 16 addressable RGB LEDs that can be controlled by Wi-Fi, or even connected to the Internet (http://wiki.protoneer.co.nz/WifiPixels).

GPIO2 is connected to the data line of the first RGB LED (pixel) in the current version. The WifiPixel can run from 5 to 12 V DC and has two power regulators on board. The first regulator is for 5 V—to run the LED power—and the secondary one regulates the 3.3 V for the ESP8266.

The used ESP-12 device can be programmed with the NodeMCU firmware, as already explained.

With this device, we can build a Wi-Fi driven display, which only needs power to operate autonomously.

Figure 9 shows the top view of the complete device. At the bottom, there are four pins to connect a console cable (described in the next chapter). The board is powered by 5 V DC and the pins are 5 V compatible, too.

Figure 9 WifiPixels

To put the WifiPixels device in boot-loader mode, one needs to hold the BOOT button down and press the RESET button. The RED status led should stay on at half brightness, indicating that the device is in boot-loader mode.

The programming itself is done, as described in Chapter 5.1. I have flashed the WifiPixels device with the already used firmware version *nodemcu_float_0.9.6_dev_20150704.bin*.

The NeoPixel Rings offered by Adafruit come with 12, 16, 24 and 60 NeoPixel LEDs, but without the ESP-12, and must be connected to an ESP8266 device by wiring (https://www.adafruit.com/search?q=neopixel).

2.3. Debug Interface

For all ESP8266 modules that have no USB to UART bridge on-board, we have to use an USB to TTL Serial Cable similar to Adafruit's USB to TTL Serial Cable—Debug/Console Cable for Raspberry Pi (Adafruit Product ID: 954, Figure 10). This console cable is responsible for serial communication and power supply.

Figure 10 USB to Serial Cable connected for Debugging

Inside the big USB plug, there is a USB<->Serial conversion chip and at the end of the 36" cable there are four wires.

There are such cables from different manufacturers. The colors of the individual ports are virtually standardized.

	Supply voltage 5 V @ 500 mA
	GND
	RX (3.3 V)
	TX (3.3 V)

3. Programming the ESP8266

For developing application programs for the ESP8266, several tool chains are available. We will concentrate on the Lua development system NodeMCU later, but I will show alternative tool chains for the sake of completeness.

3.1. ESP8266 SDK

Espressif, the vendor of the ESP8266, offers the ESP8266 SDK, which runs in a virtual machine. This time actual is ESP8266 SDK (esp_iot_sdk_v1.1.0_15_05_26), which can be downloaded from http://goo.gl/6NRhsE. The license for SDK 1.1.0 changes to the Espressif MIT license since esp_iot_sdk_v1.1.0_15_05_26.

To build the standalone SDK and toolchain, one needs a GNU/POSIX system (Linux, BSD, MacOSX, Windows with Cygwin) with the standard GNU development tools installed: gcc, binutils, flex, bison, etc.

The installation of the ESP8266 SDK is explained by https://github.com/esp8266/esp8266-wiki/wiki/Toolchain. The repository https://github.com/pfalcon/esp-open-sdk provides the integration scripts to build a complete standalone SDK (with toolchain) for software development with the Espressif ESP8266(EX) chips.

For professional software development, this is the one right way for coding. For rapid prototyping, we have effective alternatives.

3.2. Arduino IDE

The project "Arduino IDE for ESP8266" (https://goo.gl/sglsYS) brings support for the ESP8266 chip to the Arduino integrated development environment (IDE).

The ESP8266WiFi library, bundled with this project, has the same interface as the Wi-Fi Shield library, making it easy to re-use existing code and libraries.

Starting with Arduino v1.6.4, Arduino allows installation of third-party platform packages using Boards Manager. Adafruit has step-by-step instructions for that integration (https://learn.adafruit.com/add-boards-arduino-v164/). Figure 11 and Figure 12 show how to integrate new platforms into the IDE.

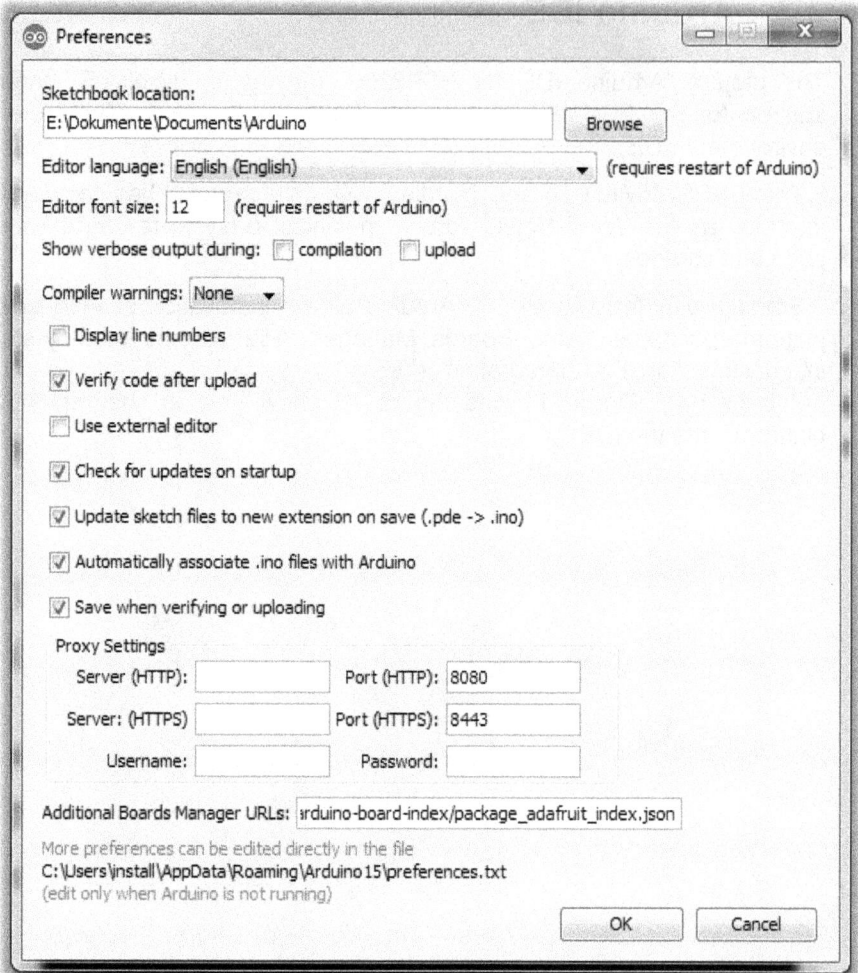

Figure 11 Integration of additional boards

The boards manager must know where to find the new platform that should be integrated. The following Adafruit boards

- Adafruit AVR Boards (Flora, Metro, Trinket, Pro Trinket, & Gemma)
- HUZZAH ESP8266 support
- Leonardo & Micro USB MIDI support (arcore)

require the entry of "https://adafruit.github.io/arduino-board-index/package_adafruit_index.json" into the field Additional Boards Manager URLs.

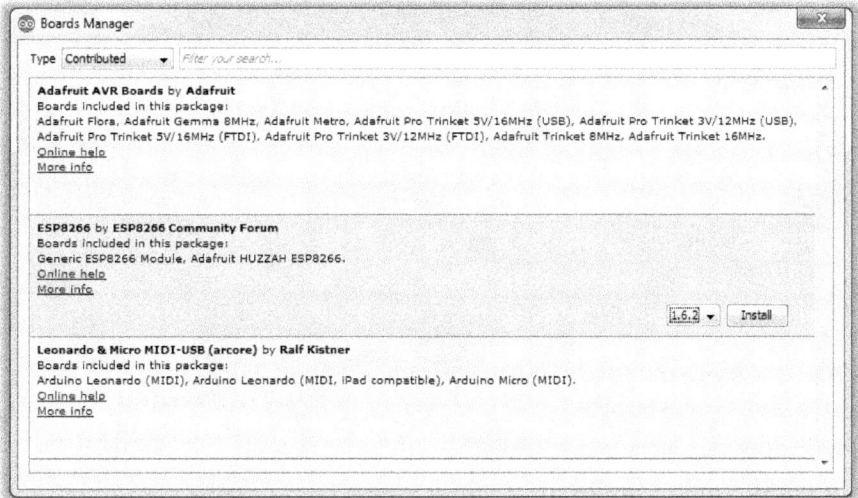

Figure 12 Boards Manager in Arduino 1.6.4

After installing the ESP8266 package and selecting the Huzzah board, we can work in the Arduino IDE as usual (Figure 13).

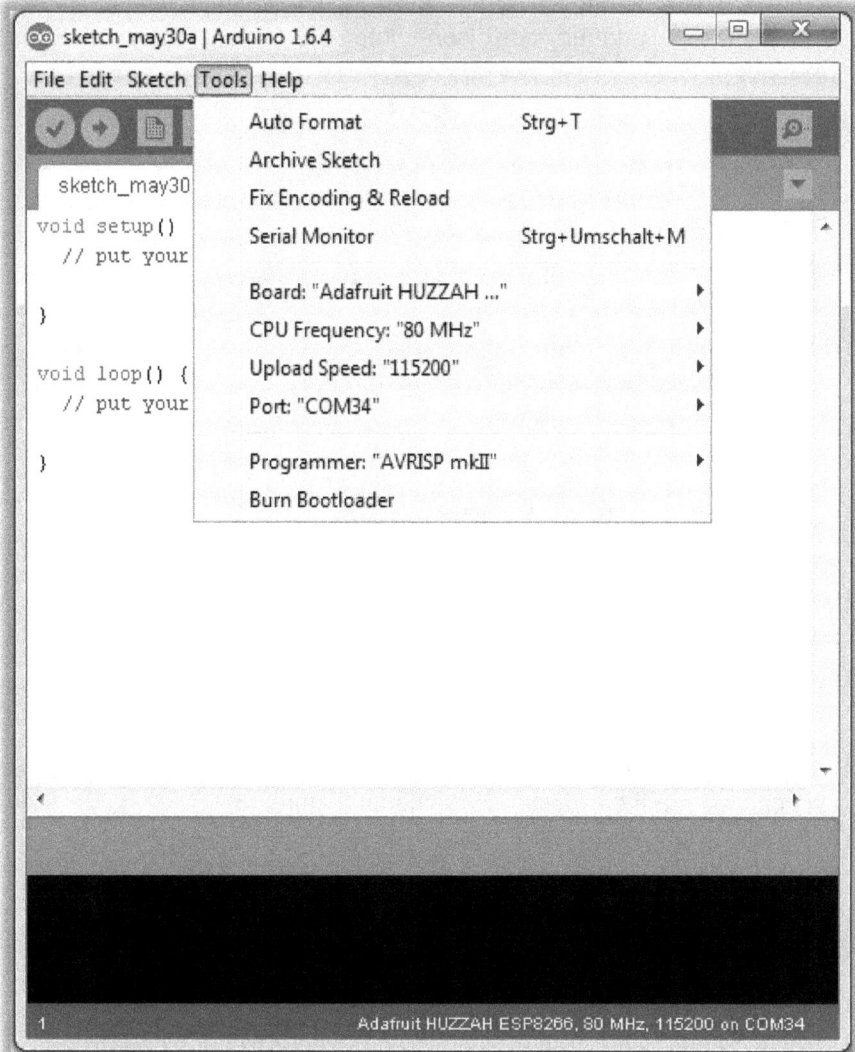

Figure 13 Huzzah Board integrated in Arduino 1.6.4 IDE

The ESP8266 Community Forum (http://goo.gl/z5Xa2L) offers support in case of questions and examples of program to study and test.

The NodeMCU modules—introduced in the next chapter—have the NodeMCU Lua interpreter preprogrammed. Using the Arduino IDE will write the generated code directly to the Flash, erasing the NodeMCU firmware. But, if one wants to go back to Lua, one will have to use the flasher to re-install it.

3.3. NodeMCU

NodeMCU is an open-source firmware and development kit that helps one prototype one's IoT device within a few Lua script lines. The firmware implemented is a Lua interpreter, which supports interactive programming.

All NodeMCU-related information is collected in https://github.com/nodemcu. The firmware repository is on https://github.com/nodemcu/nodemcu-firmware, where one will always find the actual version.

The Development Kit (NodeMCU-devkit) is based on ESP8266 and provides GPIO, PWM, I^2C, 1-Wire and 10-Bit ADC on the board.

The NodeMCU devices differ from other ESP8266 modules only through the preprogrammed firmware. Therefore, it is possible to program each other ESP8266 module with this firmware as well.

4.   Lua-based NodeMCU firmware

We have learned about the NodeMCU firmware based on Lua. It is time to explain clearly what Lua is.

4.1. Lua in general

Lua is a powerful, fast, lightweight, embeddable scripting language.

Lua combines simple procedural syntax with powerful data description constructs, based on associative arrays and extensible semantics.

Lua is dynamically typed, runs by interpreting bytecode for a register-based virtual machine, and has automatic memory management with incremental garbage collection, making it ideal for configuration, scripting, and rapid prototyping.

For a first contact with Lua, one should take a look at Wikipedia's Lua site. One can get a lot of information about the features of Lua and example code there.

The popularity of Lua is not in the top 20. If we ask the TIOBE Index for November 2015, we get the rank 29. In the RedMonk Programming Language Rankings of June 2015, we find Lua at rank 21.

Nevertheless, Lua has been used in many industrial applications (e.g., Adobe's Photoshop Lightroom), with an emphasis on embedded systems (e.g., the Gingamiddleware for digital TV in Brazil) and games (e.g., World of Warcraft and Angry Birds). Lua is currently the leading scripting language in games.

4.2. Lua Books

There is a lot of different books that cover Lua. In the past, I have especially used the following two. Roberto is one of the developers of Lua. All of them are members of the Computer Graphics Technology

Group (Tecgraf) at the Pontifical Catholic University of Rio de Janeiro, in Brazil.

Therefore, the first book is a standard work in this area. Owing to the excellent explanations, the second book is a very good addition.

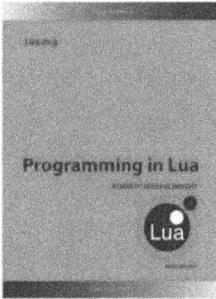

Programming in Lua
by Roberto Ierusalimschy
Lua.org, January 2013,
ISBN 859037985X

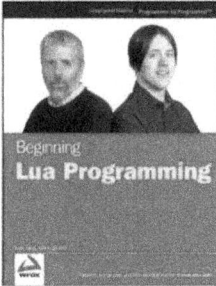

Beginning Lua Programming
by Kurt Jung and Aaron Brown
Wrox, February 2007,
ISBN 0470069171

For those who have no problems with the German language, I can recommend our book, which focuses on embedded systems:

Lua: Einsatz von Lua in Embedded Systems
by Claus Kühnel and Daniel Zwirner.
Skript Verlag Kühnel, June 2012,
ISBN 3907857151

4.3. Lua Basics

The hardware of ESP8266 is encapsulated by the NodeMCU API, and access is possible only via this interface.

The complete firmware and a lot of application examples are stored at https://github.com/nodemcu/nodemcu-firmware/.

The documentation of the complete NodeMCU language scope can be found at http://www.nodemcu.com/docs/ or the NodeMCU wiki on GitHub https://github.com/nodemcu/nodemcu-firmware/wiki/nodemcu_api_en.

As already mentioned, NodeMCU is based on Lua 5.1.4, without the debug and the os module. The function description in the supported modules can be found in the Lua manual (http://www.lua.org/manual/5.1/).

In this chapter, I will, therefore, only show a few specialties of Lua, which we will find again in Lua programs.

4.4. Dynamically Typing

The type of a variable is defined when the variable is initialized. Listing 1 shows an example. A function `p(a)` is defined there which prints the value of the variable and its type.

```
-- Dynamically Typing

function p(a)
  print(a .. " type is " .. type(a))
end

a = 123.45 ; p(a)
a = "hello"; p(a)
a = 123 + "12"; p(a)
```
Listing 1 Source code *typing.lua*

The variable `a` is initialized with the numeric value 123.45 at first and afterwards with the string "hello". Figure 14 shows call and output of the program sample *typing.lua*.

Figure 14 Call and Output of *typing.lua*

The first two assignments show the expected behavior. In the third assignment, a numeric value should be added with a number string.

If the string is convertible into a number, then Lua will do that, and the addition is allowed. If one tries to add a number and a non-numeric string, then one will get an error message: `typing.lua:10: attempt to perform arithmetic on a string value`

4.4.1. *Returning multiple variables*

In Lua, a function can have multiple return values. In Listing 2, a function `f(a, b)` is declared, which has three return values. Figure 15 shows call and output of program sample *multiple.lua*.

The function `f(a, b)` returns the first argument unchanged, the product of the first and second arguments, and the constant value 5. The first function call `f(1, 2)` return the values 1, 2, 5. The second call `f(3, 4)` therefore returns 3, 12, 5. The third call is more special. Here, the function `unpack(t)` unpacks the table `t` with its two elements serving as argument for the function `f()`. The return values are similar to the first call.

```
-- Returning multiple variables

function f(a,b)
   return a, a*b, 5
end

print(f(1,2))

a,b,c = f(3,4); print(a,b,c)
t = {1,2}; print(f(unpack(t)))
```

Listing 2 Source code *multiple.lua*

35

Figure 15 Call and Output of *multiple.lua*

4.4.2. *Variable number of arguments*

Lua offers the possibility to work with a variable number of arguments in function calls. In Listing 3, a function f(a, b, …) is declared, which has a variable number of arguments. In the first function call, we have two arguments f(1, 2), which will result in an output of 1, 2. In the second call f(1, 2, 3), the function unpack(arg) unpacks the rest of arguments and the output is 1, 2, 3. In the last function call, we have numeric and string arguments and the unpack(args) will return the string arguments to output 1, 2, "Hi", "there". Figure 16 shows call and output of program sample *arguments.lua*.

```
-- Variable number of arguments

function f(a, b, ...)
  print(a, b, unpack(arg))
end

print(f(1,2))
print(f(1,2,3))
print(f(1,2, "Hi", "there"))
```

Listing 3 Source code *arguments.lu*

36

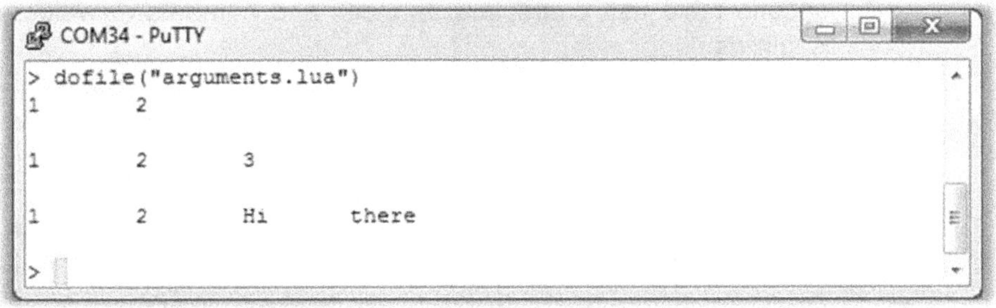

Figure 16 Call and Output of *arguments.lua*

4.4.3. Tables, Arrays and Iterators

Tables in Lua are associative arrays. An associative array is an array that uses not only numbers, but also strings and all other data types as index. Nil is not allowed.

If we use a table as an array with a numeric index, then we can use a `for` loop to go through this table. In tables with non-consecutive indexes, we have to use the iterators `ipairs()` or `pairs()`. The iterators `ipairs()` and `pairs()` always give the index and the corresponding value.

Iterators play a central role in Lua, because they allow all key value-pairs when going through a table. We will see the two possibilities: to iterate through a table (array, list).

`pairs()` iterates through all the keys in the table. However, it may not be in the exact same order one wishes. `ipairs()`, on the other hand, iterates only through numeric keys. They are both quite fast, with `pairs()` being slightly faster than `ipairs()` (if the amount of keys iterated are the same, of course). Anyway, a for loop is always faster.

In Listing 4 several tables are declared. Please verify the explanations here with the source code and the console output. Figure 17 shows call and output of program sample *table.lua*.

At first, a table with three elements is declared. In the `for`-loop, the elements are printed one after the other until the end of the table is reached. The end of the table is defined by the number of elements `#t`.

37

The second table has characters as index and numbers as value. It looks as follows:

key	value
"x"	5
"y"	7

With `pairs()` we can access each key, value-pair for print-out.

The next table has wholes—means missing entries and looks as follows.

Key	value
1	1
2	2
3	3
7	7
"string"	"hello world"

An iteration with `pairs()` outputs each key, value-pair of this table independent of its position. However, `ipairs()` stops when the first not numeric index is detected.

```lua
-- Create a table and initialize with numeric values
t = {3, 2, 1}
for i=1,#t do print(t[i]) end

-- Create a table and initialize with non-numeric indexes
t = {["x"] = 5, ["y"] = 7}
for i, v in pairs(t) do print(i, v) end

-- Create a table with "wholes"
t = {1,2}; t[3] = 3; t[7] = 7; t["string"] = "hello world"

for k,v in pairs(t) do
     print("t["..k.."] = "..v)
end

for k,v in ipairs(t) do
     print("t["..k.."] = "..v)
end
```

Listing 4 Source code *table.lua*

Figure 17 Call and Output of *table.lua*

4.4.4. Strings

The string library provides generic functions for string manipulation, such as finding and extracting substrings, and pattern matching. When indexing a string in Lua, the first character is at Position 1 (not at 0, as in C).

Indices are allowed to be negative and are interpreted as indexing backwards, from the end of the string. Thus, the last character is at position -1, and so on.

The Lua manual describes the possible string manipulations in detail (http://www.lua.org/manual/5.1/manual.html#5.4), and further examples can be found on the String Library Tutorial (http://lua-users.org/wiki/StringLibraryTutorial).

Since these detailed explanations are given, I will refrain from further explanations here.

4.5. Lua for Windows

Lua for Windows is a "batteries included environment" for the Lua scripting language on Windows.

Lua for Windows (LfW) combines Lua binaries, Lua libraries with a Lua-capable editor in a single installation package for the Microsoft Windows operating system. LfW contains everything one needs to write, run and

39

debug Lua scripts on Windows. A wide variety of libraries and examples is included; these are ready for use with Microsoft Windows.

LfW runs on Windows 2000 and newer versions of Windows. Lua and its associated libraries are also available for other operating systems; so, most scripts will be automatically cross-platform.

It is a good platform to become familiar with Lua and can be used to test functionality that has no relation to controller peripherals.

The repository is was/is on https://code.google.com/p/luaforwindows/ and moved actually to https://github.com/rjpcomputing/luaforwindows. One can download an executable program from https://github.com/rjpcomputing/luaforwindows/releases/download/v5.1.4-47/LuaForWindows_v5.1.4-47.exe as well as sources.

With the *SciTE* editor, we have an integrated development environment (IDE). In Figure 18, one can see one line Lua source code `print("Hello World!")`. After saving it as file *hw.lua*, we can press F5 to run this code.

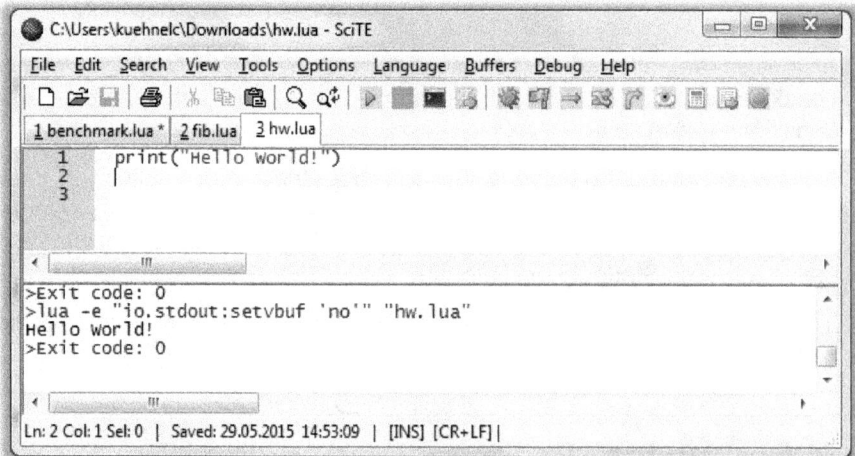

Figure 18 Hello World in LfW

One could see that LfW can be used as a playground, independent of any hardware.

4.6. Event-driven NodeMCU Programming

The previous chapters made Lua familiar as a procedural programming language. As I will show yet, the NodeMCU expects an event-driven programming approach that is very different from the conventional procedural implementation of Lua. The NodeMCU Unofficial FAQ (http://goo.gl/rt7W2h) explains some basics to understand the difference between these approaches. Important aspects of this page are reproduced here as excerpts.

Lua works embedded in a host application to provide a powerful, light-weight scripting language for use within this application. This host application can then invoke functions to execute a piece of Lua code, can write and read Lua variables, and can register C functions to be called by Lua code.

Espressif did not only design the ESP8266 SOC, but also developed and released a companion software development kit (SDK) to enable developers to build practical IoT applications for this device. The SDK is made freely available to developers in the form of binary libraries and SDK documentation. However, this is in a closed format, with no developer access to the source files, so ESP8266 applications must rely solely on the SDK API. One can see some short hints for the SDK in Chapter 3.1.

The NodeMCU firmware is an ESP8266 application and must, therefore, be layered over the ESP8266 SDK. However, the hooks and features of Lua enable it to be seamlessly integrated, without losing any of the standard Lua language features. The firmware has replaced some standard Lua modules that do not align well with the SDK structure with ESP8266 specific versions. For example, the standard IO and OS libraries do not work, but have been largely replaced by the NodeMCU node and file libraries. The debug and parts of the math libraries have also been omitted to reduce the runtime footprint.

The main impacts of the ESP8266 SDK and together with its hardware resource limitations are not in the implementation of the Lua language itself, but in how application programmers must approach the task of developing and structuring their applications.

As discussed in detail below, the SDK is non-preemptive and event-driven. Tasks can be associated with given events by using the SDK API to registering callback functions to the corresponding events. Events are queued internally within the SDK, and it then calls the associated tasks one at a time, with each task returning control to the SDK on completion.

The SDK states that if any individual task takes too long to execute, then other queued tasks can time-out; as a result, bad things start to happen.

The various libraries (net, tmr, wifi, etc.) use the SDK callback mechanism to bind Lua processing to individual events. Developers should make full use of these events to keep Lua execution sequences short.

The NodeMCU libraries act as C wrappers around registered Lua callback functions to enable these to be used as SDK tasks. One must, therefore, use an event-driven programming style in writing the NodeMCU programs (http://goo.gl/UzPuYT).

Most programmers are used to writing in a procedural style where there is a clear single flow of execution, and the program interfaces to operating system services by a set of synchronous API calls to do network I/O, etc. Whilst the logic of each individual task is procedural, this is not how one should code up NodeMCU applications.

NodeMCU implements a fully featured Lua 5.1, so that all standard Lua language constructs and data types work.

The ESP8266 uses on-chip RAM and external Flash memory connected using a dedicated SPI interface. Both of these memories are limited. The SDK and the NodeMCU firmware already use the majority of these resources. Depending on the build version and the number of modules installed, the runtime can have as little as 17 KB RAM and 40 KB Flash available for the application.

The Flash memory is formatted and made available as a SPI Flash File System (SPIFFS) through the file library. Running out of a system resource, such as RAM, will invariably cause a messy failure and system reboot.

One can choose to use a custom build reduced to the libraries one needs for one's application to significantly reduce the amount of memory. The following chapter explains the procedure.

Current versions of the ESP8266 run the SDK over the native hardware so that there is no underlying operating system to capture errors and to provide graceful failure modes; hence, system or application errors can easily "PANIC" the system, causing it to reboot. Error handling has been kept simple to save on the limited code space, and this exacerbates this tendency.

The runtime system runs in interactive mode. In this mode, it first executes the file *init.lua* when booting the system. It then "listens" to the serial port for input Lua chunks, and executes them once they are syntactically complete.

In case of an unexpected behavior of the NodeMCU application, please take a look at the document referenced for more details.

4.7. NodeMCU Custom Build

If one is experimenting with NodeMCU, one may sometimes get the issue `"not enough memory"`.

As in many embedded systems, unlimited memory is not available and that is valid for ESP8266, too, because a large portion of the available memory is occupied by the complex NodeMCU firmware.

One way out of this storage dilemma provides a customized NodeMCU firmware that contains only the modules required by the application.

If one wants to build a customized NodeMCU firmware for the ESP8266, then one can compile the firmware by oneself, or one can use an online service for that. Personally, I am excited about such an offer at http://frightanic.com/nodemcu-custom-build/.

Let us compare a standard build of the NodeMCU firmware downloadable from GitHub with a build of seven modules (by default, recommended by the tool, and shown in Figure 19); then we get the following output after calling `print(node.heap())` directly after starting a NodeMCU-devkit V1.0:

- Original-Build: 20744 Bytes
- Custom-Build according to Figure 19: 26152 Bytes

The difference of more than 5 KB helps in many situations in which programs have become somewhat larger (http://goo.gl/aOr8PB).

Comparing the relevant binaries of NodeMCU firmware versions, one clearly sees the differences in their sizes.

A custom build can be set initially in accordance with Figure 19 below. After entering one's own email address for notification of the completion of the build, the necessary modules can be selected. Finally, the field "Check the build stats" has to be clicked, and the build process starts.

NodeMCU custom builds

You customize your NodeMCU firmware and we build it. Just for you. On the spot.

Check the build stats

Your email

Enter email

It's in your own interest to leave a valid email address as we will send the build status notifications (success, failure, etc.) to this address. Most of all, however, *we need it to send you the download link* to the built binaries. Rest assured that it isn't used for anything other than running your custom build.

Select branch to build from

● master <> ○ dev <> ○ dev096 <>

Click the <> to verify on GitHub that the selected branch actually contains what you expect it to.

Select modules to include

☑ node ⊞	☐ PWM ⊞	☑ UART ⊞	☐ U8G (no docs)
☑ file ⊞	☐ I2C ⊞	☐ 1-wire ⊞	☐ WS2812 ⊞
☑ GPIO ⊞	☐ SPI ⊞	☐ bit ⊞	☐ cJSON ⊞
☑ WiFi ⊞	☑ timer ⊞	☐ MQTT ⊞	
☑ net ⊞	☐ ADC ⊞	☐ COAP (no docs)	

Click the ⊞ to go to the module documentation if you're uncertain whether you should include it or not.

We'd really like to offer some guidance as to which modules to select but the NodeMCU group doesn't provide a documented dependency matrix yet. See #386 for details.

Miscelleneous options

☐ SSL support, *required for MQTT module (build will fail if disabled, see #432)*

U8G fonts, ✓ select

font_6x10,font_chikita

keep the font list down to a minimum, if you select all modules there's room for about 8 fonts

44

Figure 19 Module Selection for customized NodeMCU Firmware

If the build is available for download, one gets a relevant notification via email.

NodeMCU custom build finished

Your NodeMCU custom build finished successfully.

You may now download The firmware:
- float: http://frightanic.com/nodemcu-custom-build/builds/nodemcu-master-7-modules-2015-06-14-15-28-24-float.bin
- integer: http://frightanic.com/nodemcu-custom-build/builds/nodemcu-master-7-modules-2015-06-14-15-28-24-integer.bin

This was built against the master branch and includes the following modules: node, file, gpio, Wifi, net, tmr, uart.
The files are guaranteed to be available for download for 24h.

Two files are available for download:

- *nodemcu-master-7-modules-2015-06-14-15-28-24-float.bin*
- *nodemcu-master-7-modules-2015-06-14-15-28-24-integer.bin*

The first file is a version that supports floating point numbers, while the second is reduced to integers.

If one installs the file *float.bin*, then the system responds with the following message after reset:

```
NodeMCU custom build by frightanic.com
  branch: master
  commit: 0ad574705d1a22b9ebc62bc198e6db9e792244e0
  SSL: false
  modules: node,file,gpio,Wifi,net,tmr,uart
  built on: 2015-06-14 15:27
  powered by Lua 5.1.4
```

Another option to reduce the memory requirements can be the compilation of the Lua source code with the command `node.compile()`.

As an example, I compiled the file *read_tmp36.lua* with the command `node.compile(„read_tmp36.lua")` and the reduction of the required memory is considerable, as the comparison of the files *read_tmp36.lua* and *read_tmp36.lc* shows:

read_tmp36.lua	534 Bytes
read_tmp36.lc	296 Bytes

The file *read_tmp36.lua* itself will be presented yet.

In any case, the result should be checked, because I found that for the compilation of the file *base64.lua,* the situation is represented differently:

base64.lua	1224 Bytes
base64.lc	1552 Bytes

From NodeMCU BBS (Bulletin Board System), I got the following explanation: "For most programming languages, the compiler (and linker) may write additional data structures to the final binary file, which will be used by the runtime when loading the binary module. The binary file may always have a better runtime performance, but not a smaller file size. If one's source file is very large, the binary file may be smaller than it" (http://bbs.nodemcu.com/t/lua-vs-lc/927).

If one knows this, then one can still decide whether operation will continue with one or the other file, and the other will be deleted from the system.

5.   NodeMCU tools

To develop NodeMCU programs, we do not need any complex toolchain.

There are two main tasks:

1.   Download the firmware
2.   Download the application program

The first task is rather rare. If one wants to change an ESP8266 module into a Lua programmable device like NodeMCU, then one has to flash the Lua firmware. In the next chapter, I will describe the procedure for that.

The second task is one step in the normal development cycle—editing, downloading, and testing until it runs without errors. This cycle will be our main task in the development of application programs.

5.1.   NodeMCU Firmware Programmer

The NodeMCU Firmware Programmer (*ESP8266Flasher*) is the tool that I use to flash the NodeMCU firmware to an ESP8266.

The repository of NodeMCU Flasher is under https://github.com/nodemcu/nodemcu-flasher. One can find executables for Win32 and Win64 there. The actual firmware can be downloaded as pre-built versions from https://github.com/nodemcu/nodemcu-firmware/tree/master/pre_build.

Normally, we have to switch the ESP8266 into Boot-loader Mode by connecting GPIO0 to GND. The NodeMCU Flasher does that for us. So we have to connect the ESP8266 module via USB to the PC and select the corresponding COM port. I wanted to update the firmware on a NodeMCU from 0.9.5 to 0.9.6 and had to connect COM33 (Figure 20).

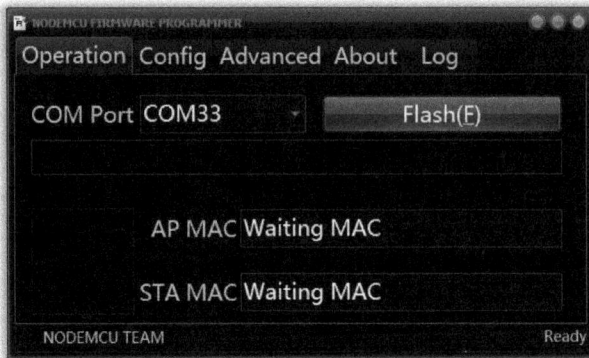

Figure 20 Selection of COM port

In the Config Tab, we can select the firmware binary to flash. The default version can be used in a situation when we want to go back to a proven state (Figure 21). Otherwise, one selects a firmware version downloaded from repository earlier.

I downloaded the new version 0.9.6 earlier and select this for the firmware update (Figure 22):

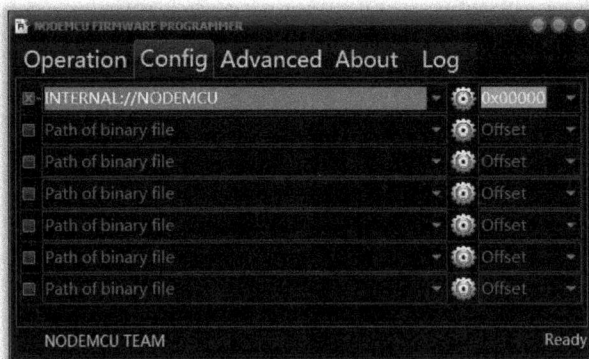

Figure 21 Selection of default firmware version

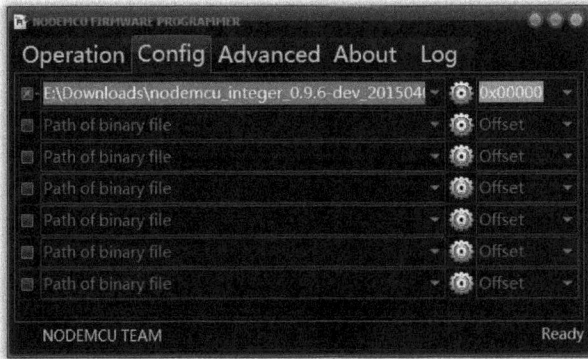

Figure 22 Selection of a new firmware version

Before we can program the new firmware, we can check the programming options. Normally, this option will be set once and will, furthermore, stay unchanged (Figure 23).

Figure 23 Programming Options

Now we are ready to start the download of the new firmware version. We have to press the flash button and wait for the downloading to finish. The progress bar keeps us informed and the green sign at bottom left signalizes success (Figure 24). Otherwise, we get a red sign.

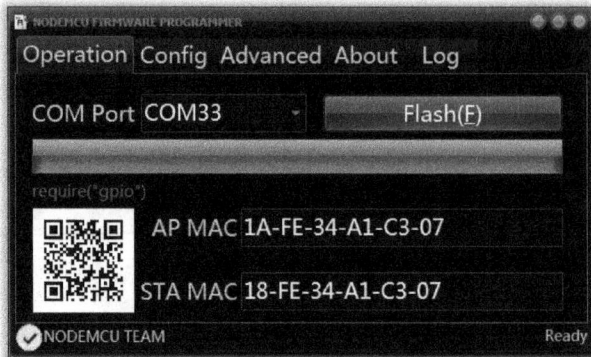

Figure 24 Firmware download

Now we are ready and want to verify the expected behavior of the updated firmware on our ESP8266 module. For this test, we need a tool, as described in the next two chapters.

5.2. ESPlorer

ESPlorer is the essential multiplatform tool for any ESP8266 developer from luatool authors, including a LUA for NodeMCU and MicroPython. It requires JAVA (SE version 7 and above) to be installed.

One can download a zip archive containing *ESPlorer* from http://esp8266.ru/esplorer-latest/?f=ESPlorer.zip.

After installation, one will have a complete IDE where one can edit Lua sources on the left side. On the right side, there is the communication window that visualizes all traffic on the serial interface (Figure 25).

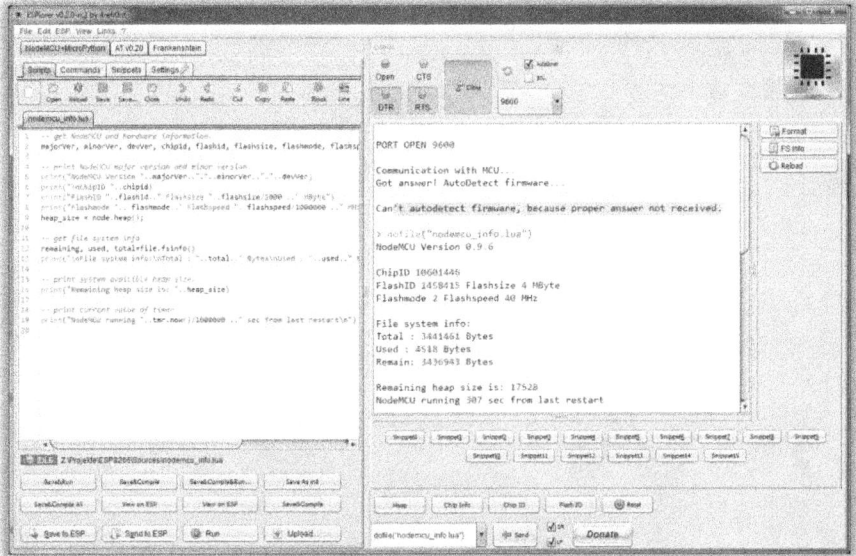

Figure 25 *ESPlorer*

5.3. NodeMCU Studio

NodeMCU Studio is a tool for downloading Lua programs to NodeMCU. Actually, it runs under Windows7 & XP (with .NET framework installed). One has to save Lua sources into the folder Lua programs, than one can run NodeMCU Studio.

NodeMCU Studio can be downloaded from https://github.com/nodemcu/nodemcu-studio-csharp.

One will have a source code window in the upper part and a communication window below (Figure 26). To edit Lua sources, one has to use an external editor like *Notepad*++, for example.

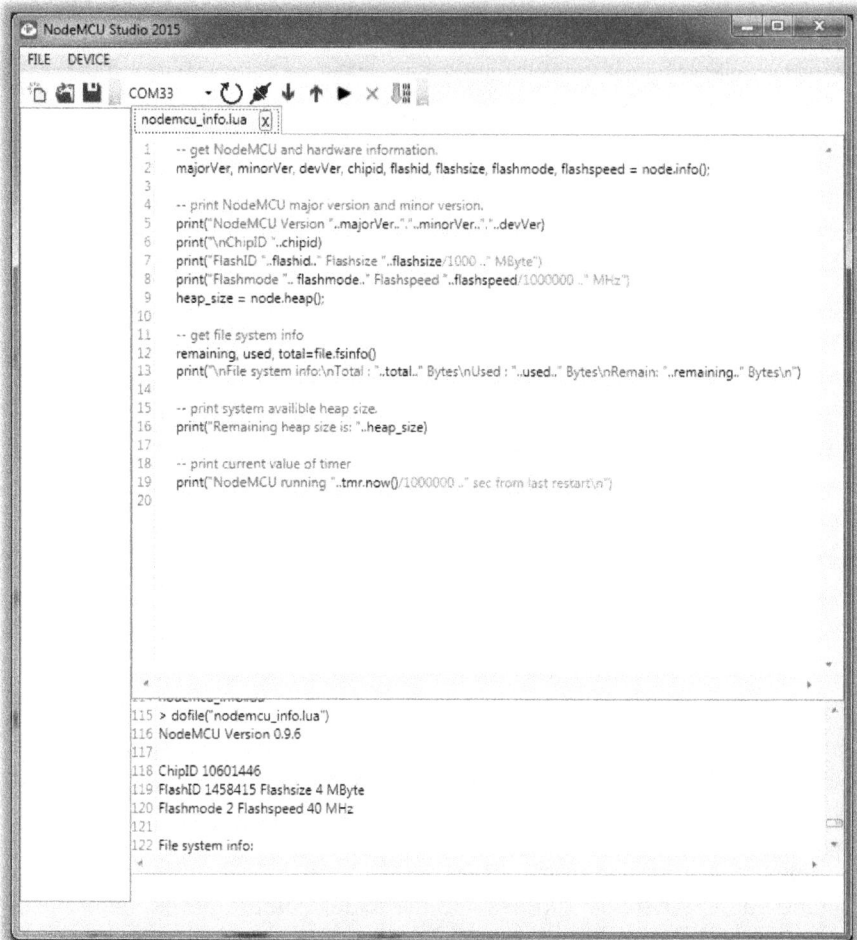

Figure 26 NodeMCU Studio

5.4. Source code Reduction by *LuaSrcDiet*

LuaSrcDiet reduces the size of Lua 5.1.x source files by aggressively removing all unnecessary whitespace and comments, optimizing constant tokens, and renaming local variables to shorter names.

LuaSrcDiet can be downloaded from http://luasrcdiet.luaforge.net/.

The 5.1.x version is being actively worked on, while the older 5.0.x version is unmaintained. The 5.1.x version should not be considered completely error-free, but currently it can reprocess its own source files without errors.

LuaSrcDiet squeezes its own (heavily commented) sources *LuaSrcDiet.lua* from 121 KB down to 28 KB.

Squeezing the sources and renaming locals can be used as a weak form of obfuscation. However, it should be noted that the structure and arrangement of the source code stays exactly the same, so one should not depend on such a weak form of obfuscation if one really requires heavy-duty obfuscation.

Calling the *LuaSrcDiet* help by `lua LuaSrcDiet.lua --help` shows us the calling options and how to use this tool (Listing 5).

```
LuaSrcDiet: Puts your Lua 5.1 source code on a diet
Version 0.11.2 (20080608)  Copyright (c) 2005-2008 Kein-Hong
Man
The COPYRIGHT file describes the conditions under which this
software may be distributed.
usage: LuaSrcDiet [options] [filenames]

example:
  >LuaSrcDiet myscript.lua -o myscript_.lua

options:
  -v, --version       prints version information
  -h, --help          prints usage information
  -o <file>           specify file name to write output
  -s <suffix>         suffix for output files (default '_')
  --keep <msg>        keep block comment with <msg> inside
  --plugin <module>   run <module> in plugin/ directory
  -                   stop handling arguments

  (optimization levels)
  --none              all optimizations off (normalizes EOLs
only)
```

```
--basic              lexer-based optimizations only
--maximum            maximize reduction of source

(informational)
--quiet              process files quietly
--read-only          read file and print token stats only
--dump-lexer         dump raw tokens from lexer to stdout
--dump-parser        dump variable tracking tables from
parser
--details            extra info (strings, numbers, locals)

features (to disable, insert 'no' prefix like --noopt-
comments):
--opt-comments       remove comments and block comments
--opt-whitespace     remove whitespace excluding EOLs
--opt-emptylines     remove empty lines
--opt-eols           all above, plus remove unnecessary
EOLs
--opt-strings        optimize strings and long strings
--opt-numbers        optimize numbers
--opt-locals         optimize local variable names
--opt-entropy        tries to reduce symbol entropy of
locals

default settings:
--opt-comments --opt-whitespace --opt-emptylines
--opt-numbers --opt-locals
```

Listing 5 *LuaScrDiet* Help Output

54

6. NodeMCU Applications

In this part of the book—the main part—various NodeMCU applications are considered, which can then be combined into IoT applications.

Owing to the ease of use, most of the programming examples are tested on a NodeMCU-devkit.

6.1. Simple Lua Utilities

By presenting simple Lua utilities, I will introduce the Lua-based NodeMCU syntax. These utilities serve as useful tools as well.

6.1.1. Program init.lua

If a new firmware is installed and no other programs are saved in the flash memory, then NodeMCU outputs after start-up `lua: cannot open init.lua`.

The file *init.lua* is called during each restart and initializes the system. Usually, I work with the following file (Listing 6).

```
--load credentials
--SID and PassWord should be saved according wireless router in
use
dofile("credentials.lua")

--init.lua
print("set up wifi mode")
wifi.setmode(wifi.STATION)
wifi.sta.config(SSID,PASSWORD)
wifi.sta.connect()
tmr.alarm(1, 1000, 1, function()
    if wifi.sta.getip()== nil then
        print("IP unavailable, Waiting...")
```

```
    else
        tmr.stop(1)
        print("Config done, IP is "..wifi.sta.getip())
--        dofile("myfile.lua")
    end
end)
```

Listing 6 Source code *init.lua* (Basis)

At first, the file *credentials.lua* is loaded. In this file, I hide all login data, such as user names, passwords and other information, which should not be published when source code is shared.

Listing 7 shows the notation of login data for the respective WLAN that must be adapted to one's own conditions. It is also possible to save login data for further services there. I will do that repeatedly.

```
-- Credentials
SSID = "Your SSID"
PASSWORD = "Your Password"
```

Listing 7 Source code *credentials.lua*

If the login information is known, then the connection can be established to the WLAN. The three instructions from the Wi-Fi module take over the connection. The IP address will be delivered by the router via DHCP.

A timer queries each second the IP address provided by the router until it is no longer `nil`. Is a value assigned to this address, then the timer can be stopped, and the IP address will be issued.

Although commented here, the file *init.lua* can also start an application program (`dofile("myfile.lua")`).

If one wants to work with a fixed IP address, then one would have set it through the code lines after `wifi.sta.connect()` explicitly.

```
wifi.sta.connect()

cfg = { ip      ="192.168.1.111",
        netmask="255.255.255.0",
        gateway="192.168.1.1"  }

wifi.sta.setip(cfg)
```

If one has an error in the file *init.lua,* or in the file possibly called *myfile.lua,* that leads to an endless loop with repeated reboots, then the ESP8266 has to be flashed with fresh NodeMCU firmware. In such cases, it is helpful to have an interrupt option within the file *init.lua.*

In the post "ESP8266/NodeMCU: Methods of Interrupting init.lua During Boot" (https://goo.gl/t1MldS), different ways are offered for that; I will present one of those here.

After starting the ESP8266, the execution of the user program can be delayed by a time that can be used to interrupt the startups. The file *init.lua* would then be supplemented by the following lines.

```
function startup()
  print("Running Startup…")
  dofile("myfile.lua")
end

print("You have 5 seconds to abort Startup")
tmr.alarm(0,5000,0,startup)
```

Within these five seconds, on error the file *init.lua* must be deleted to avoid a restart. To those who need more time to tap the required commands, the IDE helps here. The entire command sequences can be put on the Snippets fields, such as:

```
file.remove("init.old")
file.rename("init.lua", "init.old")
```

The faulty file *init.lua* is renamed as *init.old*, where the old file *init.old* was previously deleted. Now the file *init.lua* can be edited, can be saved into flash memory, and can be retested.

If everything is running without any errors, then the time delay and, with it, the possibility of interruption can again be removed.

Listing 8 shows the enhanced file *init.lua.*

```
--load credentials
--SID and PassWord should be saved according wireless router in
use
dofile("credentials.lua")
```

```
function startup()
    if file.open("init.lua") == nil then
      print("init.lua deleted")
    else
      print("Running")
      file.close("init.lua")
--   dofile(myfile.lua)
    end
end

--init.lua
print("set up wifi mode")
wifi.setmode(wifi.STATION)
wifi.sta.config(SSID,PASSWORD)
wifi.sta.connect()
tmr.alarm(1, 1000, 1, function()
    if wifi.sta.getip()== nil then
        print("IP unavailable, Waiting...")
    else
        tmr.stop(1)
        print("Config done, IP is "..wifi.sta.getip())
        print("You have 5 seconds to abort Startup")
        print("Waiting...")
        tmr.alarm(0,5000,0,startup)
    end
 end)
```

Listing 8 Source code *init.lua* (enhanced function)

6.1.2. Program nodemcu_info.lua

The program *nodemcu_info.lua* provides some system information to us. Listing 9 shows how to get system information by calling node.info(), file.fsinfo(), node.heap() and tmr.now() and preparing the results for console output.

Figure 27 shows the console output of the information collected by the program *nodemcu_info.lua*.

```
-- Title   : Lists NodeMCU and hardware information
-- Date    : 2015-07-30
-- Id      : nodemcu_info.lua
-- Firmware: nodemcu_float_0.9.6-dev_20150704
-- Created : Claus Kuehnel

-- get NodeMCU and hardware information.
majorVer, minorVer, devVer, chipid, flashid, flashsize,
```

58

```
flashmode, flashspeed = node.info()

-- print NodeMCU major version and minor version.
print("NodeMCU Version
"..majorVer..".".."..minorVer..".".."..devVer)
print("\nChipID "..chipid)
print("FlashID "..flashid.." Flashsize "..flashsize/1000 .."
MByte")
print("Flashmode ".. flashmode.." Flashspeed
"..flashspeed/1000000 .." MHz")

-- get file system info
remaining, used, total=file.fsinfo()
print("\nFile system info:\nTotal : "..total.." Bytes\nUsed
: "..used.." Bytes\nRemain: "..remaining.." Bytes\n")

-- print system available heap size.
heap_size = node.heap()
print("Remaining heap size is: "..heap_size)

-- print current value of timer
print("NodeMCU running "..tmr.now()/1000000 .." sec from
last restart\n")
```
Listing 9 Source code *nodemcu_info.lua*

```
NodeMCU Version 0.9.6

ChipID 10554992
FlashID 1458415 Flashsize 4.096 MByte
Flashmode 2 Flashspeed 40 MHz

File system info:
Total : 3396281 Bytes
Used : 24096 Bytes
Remain: 3372185 Bytes

Remaining heap size is: 25328
NodeMCU running 8.742098 sec from last restart
```

Figure 27 Listing System Info

6.1.3. Program dir.lua

The command `dir` lists in DOS and Windows programs the content of directories of a storage medium.

During development and test of Lua programs for NodeMCU, one or the other program is loaded into the memory of the ESP8266. In order to maintain an overview, it is desirable to list the content of memory, as required.

The program *dir.lua,* shown in Listing 10, reads the content of the flash memory and outputs it in the usual way (file name, file size) to the console (Figure 28).

```
-- Title   : List all files
-- Date    : 2015-06-01
-- Id      : dir.lua
-- Firmware: nodemcu_float_0.9.6-dev_20150406
-- Found at: https://github.com/annejan/nodemcu-lua-watch
-- Modified: Claus Kuehnel

-- Lists all files stored on ESP8266 device
print("Listing all files on ESP8266 device:")
l = file.list();
for k,v in pairs(l) do
  print(k.. "\t"..v.." Bytes")
end
l = nil
```
Listing 10 Source code *dir.lua*

The function `file.list()` builds a table `l` containing file name and file size in pairs. The iterator `pairs(l)` provides these data for output line by line. At last, the table is assigned with `nil`, i.e., practically deleted.

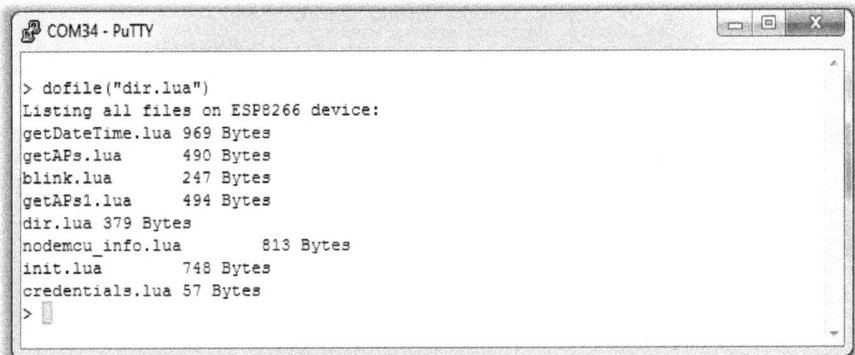

```
> dofile("dir.lua")
Listing all files on ESP8266 device:
getDateTime.lua 969 Bytes
getAPs.lua      490 Bytes
blink.lua       247 Bytes
getAPs1.lua     494 Bytes
dir.lua 379 Bytes
nodemcu_info.lua        813 Bytes
init.lua        748 Bytes
credentials.lua 57 Bytes
>
```

Figure 28 Listing the content of flash memory

6.1.4. Program getAPs.lua

All visible access points (AP) can be scanned using the function `wifi.sta.getap(listap)` and provided as a table. The function is quite complex; therefore, one has to necessarily look in case of any adaptions to the firmware description.

Listing 11 shows the program *getAPs.lua* and Figure 29 the console output of this function.

```
-- Title   : Lists Access Points
-- Date    : 2015-07-30
-- Id      : getAPs.lua
-- Firmware: nodemcu_float_0.9.6-dev_20150704
-- Created : Claus Kuehnel

-- print ap list
function listap(t)
  print("\nVisible Access Points:")
  print("SSID Authmode RSSI  BSSID   Channel")
  for ssid,v in pairs(t) do
    authmode, rssi, bssid, channel = string.match(v,
"(%d),(-?%d+),(%x%x:%x%x:%x%x:%x%x:%x%x:%x%x),(%d+)")
    print(ssid,authmode,rssi,bssid,channel)
  end
end

wifi.sta.getap(listap)
```

Listing 11 Source code *getAPs.lua*

61

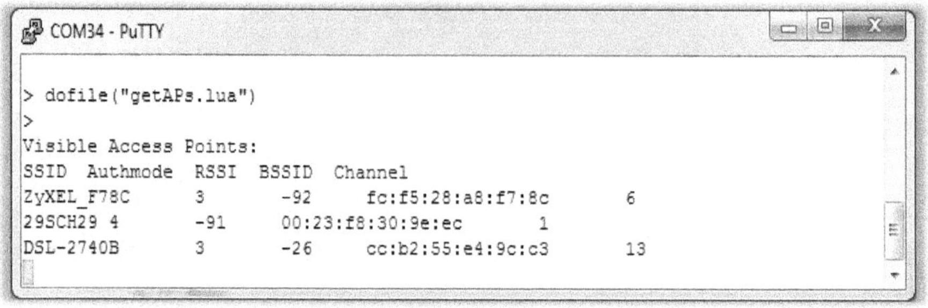

Figure 29 Output of all visible Access Points

At the time of the call, three access points are visible. My AP has the SSID DSL 2740B and transmits on Channel 13. The Received Signal Strength Indicator (RSSI) indicates the quality of the connection between ESP8266 and the Access Point. According to the following table, an RSSI value of -26 dB is an indicator for an excellent wireless connection.

RSSI Range	Quality of Signal
Better than -40 dB	excellent
-40 dB to -55 dB	very good
-55 dB to -70 db	good
-70 dB to -80 dB	poor
-80 dB and below	unstable

6.1.5. Program getDateTime

The NodeMCU modules do not have a real-time clock (RTC). From the node, reported events must be linked with date and/or time information later, or the node gets this information directly from a server on the net.

Listing 12 shows the program *getDateTime.lua*—this queries a server and determines date and time from the answer of that server. Here, we query a Google server. But, in practice, it may also be any other server that has a stable time base.

```
-- Title    : Google Time
-- Date     : 2015-08-08
-- Id       : getDateTime.lua
-- Firmware: nodemcu_float_0.9.6-dev_20150406
-- Found at: http://benlo.com/esp8266/esp8266Projects.html
-- Modified: Claus Kuehnel

conn = net.createConnection(net.TCP, 0)

conn:on("connection",function(conn, payload)
conn:send("HEAD / HTTP/1.1\r\n"..
          "Host: google.com\r\n"..
          "Accept: */*\r\n"..
          "User-Agent: Mozilla/4.0 (compatible; esp8266
Lua;)"..
          "\r\n\r\n")
          end)
conn:on("receive", function(conn, payload)
    date = string.sub(payload,string.find(payload,"Date: ")
          +6,string.find(payload,"Date: ")+35)
    wday = string.sub(date, 1, 3)
    day = string.sub(date, 6, 7)
    month = string.sub(date, 9, 11)
    year = string.sub(date, 13, 16)
    hour = string.sub(date, 18,19)
    min = string.sub(date, 21, 22)
    sec = string.sub(date, 24,26)
--    print(payload)
    print("\n"..day..". "..month.."
"..year.."\t"..hour..":"..min..":"..sec.." GMT")
    hour = tostring(tonumber(hour) + 2)
    print(day..". "..month.."
"..year.."\t"..hour..":"..min..":"..sec.." CEST")
    conn:close()
    end)
conn:connect(80,'google.com')
```

Listing 12 Source code *getDateTime.lua*

If the connection to the server is established, then the HEAD information is sent. The server will send some data back that is stored in the variable `payload`. This string is decomposed afterward with respect to date and time, and output via the console.

Figure 30 shows the output of the variable `payload` followed by the time information. In this way, the decomposition of the strings can be tracked well.

For the actual time query, the issue of payload is not of interest and can be commented out. Figure 31 shows the output thus reduced by date and time.

In both cases, the Greenwich Mean Time (GMT) was still converted into Central European Summer Time (CEST).

```
COM34 - PuTTY                                                    _  □  X
dofile("getDateTime.lua")
> HTTP/1.1 302 Found
Cache-Control: private
Content-Type: text/html; charset=UTF-8
Location: http://www.google.ch/?gfe_rd=cr&ei=MqrGVfntMOmX8QekoanwBg
Content-Length: 258
Date: Sun, 09 Aug 2015 01:17:38 GMT
Server: GFE/2.0
Alternate-Protocol: 80:quic,p=0


09. Aug 2015     01:17:38  GMT
09. Aug 2015     3:17:38  CEST
```

Figure 30 Query the Google Servers

```
COM34 - PuTTY                                                    _  □  X
dofile("getDateTime.lua")
>
09. Aug 2015     01:20:09  GMT
09. Aug 2015     3:20:09  CEST
```

Figure 31 Query Date and Time

6.2. Connecting Peripherals

Peripherals—a synonym for sensors and actors—are equipped with a variety of interfaces and the communication with a microcontroller sometimes requires additional circuitry. The way of connecting peripherals to NodeMCU devices and/or ESP8266 is explained in this chapter.

6.2.1. Digital Output

The digital output is used to control digital output stages or relays, and can control various switching states this way.

The program *dio.lua* initializes Pin D8 (of a NodeMCU-devkit) as a digital output and toggles a connected LED each second (Listing 13).

Figure 32 shows how to connect an LED to the NodeMCU-devkit. The value of the series resistor is not critical. An ESP8266 output can drive 12 mA maximum.

One can calculate the series resistor by the following formula:

$$R = \frac{V_{CC} - V_{OL} - V_F}{I_F}$$

V_{CC} here means the 3.3 V supply voltage of the NodeMCU, V_F is the forward voltage of the LED, and V_{OL} the output voltage at an output pin switched to Lo-potential.

With a resistor value of 220 Ω, we get a forward current of 5 mA for the LED (R = (3.3 − 0.2 − 2.0) V /5 mA = 220 Ω). I have used 0.2 V as voltage V_{OL} and 2.0 V for V_F (Red LED). Some hints on LEDs are provided in Chapter 0.

If one is willing to experiment a little bit, then one will find a web-based calculator at http://goo.gl/5clBYX.

U1

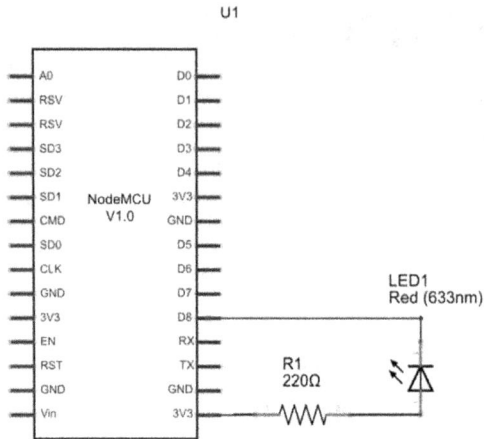

Figure 32 Controlling a LED

Now, back to the program sample *dio.lua* again.

After defining the output to be used for the LED, this output must be configured with the command `gpio.mode(LED,gpio.OUTPUT)`. After that, I defined the function `toggle_output(pin)`. Each time this function is called the variable `state` changes between 0 and 1 and switches the output pin Hi or Lo.

Timer0 serves as a time base and calls each second the function `toggle_output(LED)` switching the LED in the opposite state. The timer can be stopped by calling `tmr.stop(0)`, which stops the blinking as well.

The relationship between IO index and ESP8266 pin numbering is described in Appendix 8.1. The NodeMCU-devkit use the IO index (0 = D0 etc.), while the ESP8266 modules must be addressed by ESP pin numbers.

```
-- Title    : Digital Output
-- Date     : 2015-06-01
-- Id       : dio.lua
-- Firmware: nodemcu_float_0.9.6-dev_20150406
-- Created : Claus Kuehnel info[at]ckuehnel.ch
```

```
-- Connect LED & resistor to Pin8 (D8) of NodeMCU
LED = 8 -- D8

state = 0

-- set gpio 0 as output.
gpio.mode(LED, gpio.OUTPUT)

function toggle_output(pin)
    if state == 0 then
        gpio.write(LED, gpio.HIGH)
    else
        gpio.write(LED, gpio.LOW)
    end

    state = (state + 1)%2
end

-- toggles LED at pin 8 every 1000ms
tmr.alarm(0, 1000, 1, function() toggle_output(LED) end )

print("LED connected to Pin8 will be toggled every second")
print("Stop this by tmr.stop(0)")
```
Listing 13 Source code *dio.lua*

Figure 33 shows the process of running the program *dio.lua* and stopping the timer to stop the blinking of the LED afterward.

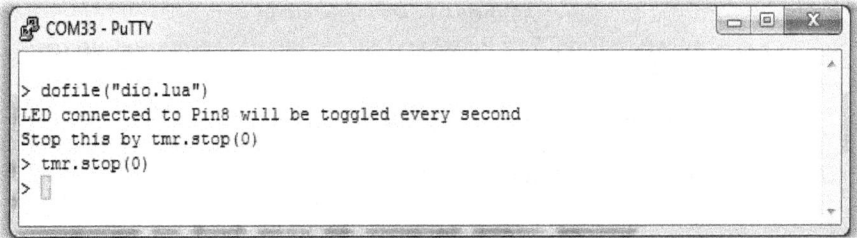

Figure 33 Start and Stop *dio.lua*

6.2.2. Digital Input

For digital input, the logical state on a pin declared as a digital input is queried.

Figure 34 shows a pushbutton connected to pin D7, additionally to the LED connected to pin D8.

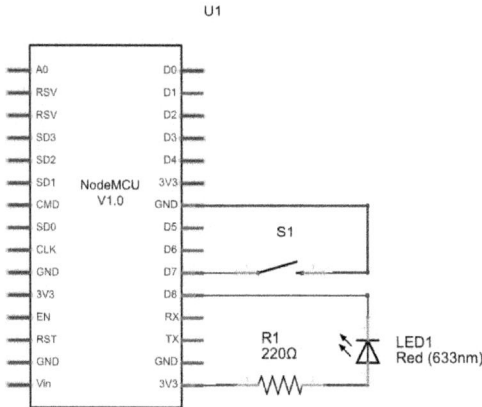

Figure 34 Digital IO

In program *dio1.lua* (Listing14), Pin D8 is initialized unchanged as digital output while Pin D7 is initialized as digital input with pull-up resistor by the command `gpio.mode(IN, gpio.INPUT, gpio.PULLUP)`. Now we can connect a pushbutton from this input to GND. If the pushbutton is pressed, the digital input is Lo; otherwise, it will be Hi by the pull-up resistor. The function `read_input(IN)` queries this digital input.

If there is a change in the input state, the detected state is printed out to the console and visualized by the LED connected to Pin D8.

A timer again queries the input state each second. These periodic queries will be stopped by stopping the timer (`tmr.stop(0)`) again.

```
-- Title    : Digital In/Output
-- Date     : 2015-06-07
-- Id       : dio1.lua
-- Firmware: nodemcu_float_0.9.6-dev_20150406
-- Created : Claus Kuehnel info[at]ckuehnel.ch

-- Connect LED & resistor to Pin8 (D8) of NodeMCU
-- Connect Switch to Pin7 (D7) of NodeMCU

LED = 8 -- D8
IN  = 7 -- D7

old_state = 1

-- set gpio 8 as output.
gpio.mode(LED, gpio.OUTPUT)

-- set gpio 7 as input w/ pullup
gpio.mode(IN, gpio.INPUT, gpio.PULLUP)

function read_input(pin)
    state = gpio.read(IN)
    if state ~= old_state then
        old_state = state
        print("State = "..state)
        if state == 1 then
            gpio.write(LED, gpio.LOW)
        else
            gpio.write(LED, gpio.HIGH)
        end
    end
end

-- input pin is queried every 1000ms
tmr.alarm(0, 1000, 1, function() read_input(IN) end )

print("If input state changes LED connected to Pin8 will
change too")
print("Stop this by tmr.stop(0)")
```

Listing 14 Source code *dio1.lua*

Figure 35 shows the process of running the program *dio1.lua* and the console output after changing the input state.

```
COM33 - PuTTY                                    _ □ X

> dofile("dio1.lua")
If input state changes LED connected to Pin8 will change too
Stop this by tmr.stop(0)
> State = 0
State = 1
State = 0
State = 1
```

Figure 35 Querying the state on pin D7

6.2.3. Ultrasonic Distance Sensor HC-SR04

The ultrasonic distance sensor HC-SR04 provides a non-contact distance measurement function in a range between 2 cm and 400 cm. The ranging accuracy can reach 3 mm. The sensor contains an ultrasonic transmitter, a receiver and a control circuit. Figure 36 shows the sensor device and its connectors. The sensor is powered with 5 V DC (VCC, GND).

Figure 36 Ultrasonic Distance Sensor HC-SR04

The measuring sequence is started by a pulse at Trig input for at least 10 µs high level signal. After that, eight 40 kHz pulses are sent, and detect whether there is a pulse signal back. The pulse length at Echo output is the time from sending ultrasonic to returning. The measured distance can be calculated by

70

$$d = \frac{t_{Hi} \times v_{US}}{2}$$

In the formula above, t_{Hi} is the pulse length of the Echo signal and v_{US} the ultrasonic speed.

Figure 37 shows the HC-SR04 signals in action with the relevant signal description. For further details, please take a look into the HC-SR04 data sheet (http://goo.gl/LNeG0C).

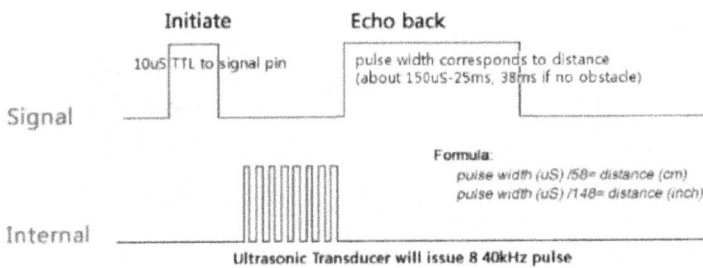

Figure 37 HC-SR04 Signals

The program for distance measurement has two separate functions. At first, it must generate the trigger pulse to start the measurement sequence and afterward, the Hi phase of the echo signal must be measured. Listing 15 shows the program *sonar.lua* implementing these functions.

At the beginning of the program, some constants are defined. The Trig input of the HC-SR04 sensor is connected to Pin D4 and the Echo output to Pin D5. These IOs were configured later.

The constants CM and INCH are conversion factors for the distance unit. In this case, here the instruction DIM = CM selects a distance output in cm.

For pulse measurement, I use the interrupt mode here. This way, I avoid blocking the system, when no falling edge will be received at Pin D5. Waiting to long for an edge on an input line provokes the system to crash.

The instruction `gpio_write = gpio.write` reduces the runtime of the function `gpio.write`. By this mean, the function `send_trigger()` generates a trigger impulse of 140 µs duration. A timer calls the function `send_trigger()` each second.

The function `measure()` is the interrupt handler for the GPIO interrupt. A rising edge at Pin D4 interrupts and calls this handler (`gpio.trig(SONAR, "up", measure)`.

The starting time is saved and the edge for the next interrupt is switched to falling (`"down"`). If the falling edge is detected, then the stop time can be saved. From both times, the duration of the Echo pulse is determined. This time is converted into a distance with the selected unit cm or inch, and printed as floating point number to the console.

One can test this newly created distance measuring system by moving one's hand in front of the sensor, and one will see the changing result.

```
-- Title   : HC-SR04 Distance Measurement
-- Date    : 2015-11-03
-- Author  : Claus Kuehnel
-- Id      : sonar.lua
-- Firmware: NodeMCU custom build by frightanic.com; branch:
dev096

TRIG  = 4
SONAR = 5
CM = 58 -- for cm
INCH = 148 -- for inch

DIM = CM

start = 0
if DIM == CM then
  dim = "cm"
elseif DIM == INCH then
  dim = "inch"
else
  print("set dimension to cm")
  dim = "cm"
  DIM = CM
end

gpio.mode(TRIG,gpio.OUTPUT)
gpio.write(TRIG, gpio.LOW)

gpio.mode(SONAR,gpio.INT) --, gpio.PULLDOWN)
```

```
function measure(level)
  if level == 1 then
    tstart = tmr.now()
    gpio.trig(SONAR, "down")
  else
    distance = (tmr.now() - tstart)/DIM
    if distance < 300 then
      print(string.format("Distance = %.1f %s", distance,
dim))
    else
      print("No good signal")
    end
    gpio.trig(SONAR, "up")
  end
end

gpio.trig(SONAR, "up", measure)

gpio_write = gpio.write -- to speed up gpio.write

function send_trigger(out)
  gpio_write(out, gpio.HIGH)
--  tmr.delay(10)
  gpio_write(out, gpio.LOW) -- 140 us pulse instead of 260
us
end

tmr.alarm(0, 1000, 1, function() send_trigger(TRIG) end)
```
Listing 15 Source code *sonar.lua*

6.2.4. Analog Input

The ESP8266 device has a 10-bit analog-to-digital converter (ADC). The voltage to be detected is to lead to the input A0 (TOUT). It should be noted that the input voltage range of the ESP8266 ADC extends from about 0 to 1000 mV only.

Some modules have a voltage divider to adjust the input voltage range to the 3.3 V supply voltage. A look into the data sheet provides clarity here.

For the modules considered here, only the NodeMCU-devkit v2 has this voltage divider on-board. The direct analog input A0 (TOUT) is additionally available outside.

The output signal of the temperature sensor TMP36 (Analog Devices) extends about a temperature range of -40°C to +125°C (-40°F to +257°F) from 0.1 V to 1.750 V with a gradient of 10 mV/K and a value of 750 mV @ 25°C (77°F).

Figure 38 shows the connection of the temperature sensors to the NodeMCU-devkit. A jumper is used to select the voltage range. The voltage divider R1/R2 is responsible for the adjustment of the voltage range to the ADC's input voltage range when no on-board voltage divider exists.

$$U_{ADC} = \frac{R_1}{R_1 + R_2} \cdot U_{TMP36} = 0.577 \cdot U_{TMP36}$$

This quotient has to be considered in the result output.

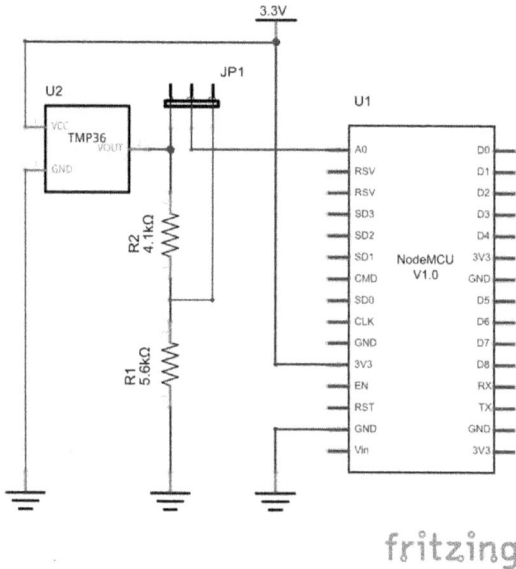

Figure 38 TMP36 connected to NodeMCU-devkit

Owing to the comfortable application programming interface (API), the program for reading the temperature sensor TMP36 is very simple (see Listing 16).

74

The function `adc.read(0)` returns the ADC output value representing the voltage at input A0 (TOUT). After scaling the value of the variable, `volt` corresponds to the measured temperature and is ready for printout.

```lua
-- Title   : Read TMP36 temperature sensor
-- Author  : Claus Kuehnel
-- Date     : 2015-06-01
-- Id       : read_tmp36.lua
-- Firmware: nodemcu_float_0.9.6-dev_20150406
-- Copyright © 2015 Claus Kuehnel info[at]ckuehnel.ch

-- TMP36 output via voltage divider to TOUT (4.3 k/5.6 k)

print("Reading TMP36 sensor")

volt = adc.read(0)
--volt = 1000              -- 125°C
--volt = 750*1000/1750 -- 25°C
--volt = 500*1000/1750 -- 0°C
--volt = 100*1000/1750 -- -40°C

volt = ((volt*1.75)-500)/10
print("Temperature = "..volt.." °C")
```

Listing 16 Source code *read_tmp36.lua*

Figure 39 shows the call of the program *read_tmp36.lua* and its console output of the measured temperature.

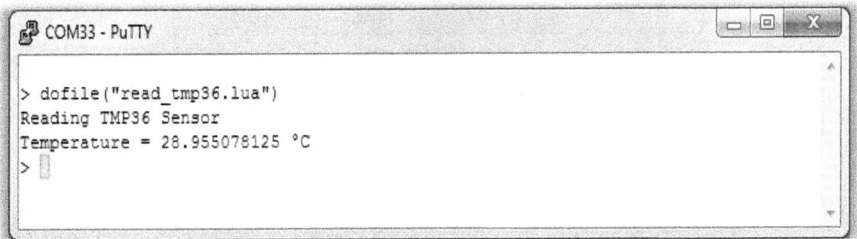

```
> dofile("read_tmp36.lua")
Reading TMP36 Sensor
Temperature = 28.955078125 °C
>
```

Figure 39 Measuring temperature by TMP36

6.2.5. Analog Output

The ESP8266 has one analog input. As analog output, we can use PWM. The mean value of the output voltage can be controlled by the duty of the PWM output signal. This kind of control is used to control the brightness of LEDs, the power of heating elements, speed control of DC motors—and more.

If one wishes to measure the output voltage, one would have to filter the PWM output by a RC filter.

For a simple RC filter, the time constant can be calculated by the following equation (to get an attenuation of 20 dB for the PWM frequency):

$$\tau = R * C = \frac{10}{2\pi * f_{PWM}}$$

If we can use a high PWM frequency, then the time constant will be low. NodeMCU allows a PWM clock of maximum 1,000 Hz. A PWM clock frequency of 1 kHz needs a time constant of 1.59 ms (cut-off frequency of the filter 100 Hz) to get a filter effect. Please see Table 3 for the details.

| | | Cut-off frequency | | |
		10 Hz	100 Hz	1000 Hz
Ripple	$\Delta V_{pk\text{-}pk}$ (Duty=0.5)	51 mV	514 mV	3 V
Settling time	t_r (w/o ripple)	36 ms	3.6 ms	0.36 ms

Table 3 PWM Filter

On choosing a higher time constant (lower cut-off frequency), the filter effect and the settling time will increase. Choosing a lower time constant (higher cut-off frequency) reduces the effect of filtering and the settling time.

One has to find the right compromise in relation to one's application. The PWM Filter Calculator, which can be found at hthttp://goo.gl/wJtBz0, is a good instrument to find an optimal value for the components of the filter.

Apart from the simple RC filter (1st order), one can look for a higher order filter as well. There is a lot of proposals in the web. Please see http://goo.gl/3p9K6R, http://goo.gl/53BZjl, http://goo.gl/fPmAs6, for example.

To test the PWM output, we can connect the filtered PWM output to the analog input. As filter, a simple RC combination with a time constant of 1.6 ms is used, as Figure 40 shows.

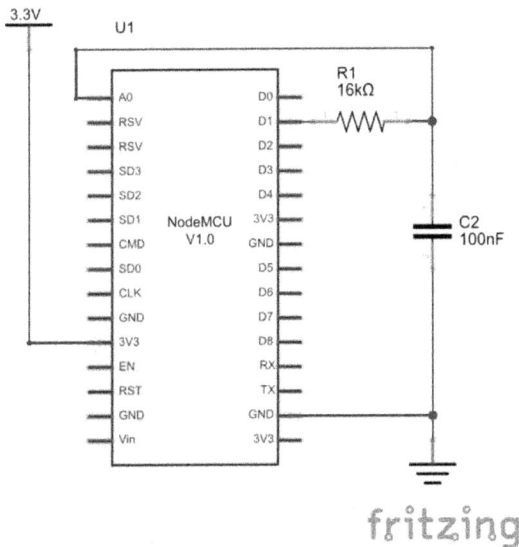

Figure 40 Filtered PWM output connected to analog input

Listing 17 shows the source code of the program sample *adda.lua*. The PWM output is defined by `pwm.setup(PWMOUT, 1000, DUTY)` with `PWM = 1` and `DUTY = 512`, which means a PWM frequency of 1 kHz and a duty cycle of 512/1024 = 0.5. The instruction `pwm.start()` activates the output signal.

After this initialization, we read back the PWM frequency and the duty for a formatted output. To reduce the digits after the decimal point to three, we can take the function `string.format("%.3f", number)` as used in the output of the duty cycle.

We can now go into the loop to set the PWM duty, wait for it to settle, and read the analog-to-digital converter (ADC) followed by a formatted printout.

The function `print(string.format("%4d\t%4d\t%4d",duty, analog, duty - analog))` prints the data in three columns separated by tabs each. In this way, we can get an output of the whole program, as listed in Figure 41.

```lua
PWMOUT = 1
DUTY = 512
STEP = 64

-- set pin 1 as pwm output, frequency is 1000Hz, duty cycle
is half.
pwm.setup(PWMOUT, 1000, DUTY)
pwm.start(PWMOUT)

print("PWM Frequency = "..pwm.getclock(PWMOUT).." Hz")
print("PWM Duty      =
 "..string.format("%.3f",pwm.getduty(PWMOUT)/1024))

print("DAC \tADC \tDAC-ADC")
print("=======================")
for duty = 0, 1023, STEP do
  pwm.setduty(PWMOUT, duty)
  tmr.delay(2000 * 1000)
  analog = adc.read(0)
  print(string.format("%4d\t%4d\t%4d",duty, analog, duty -
analog))
end
```

Listing 17 Source code *adda.lua*

```
> dofile("adda.lua");
PWM Frequency = 1000 Hz
PWM Duty      = 0.500
DAC      ADC       DAC-ADC
========================
   0        0          0
  64       63          1
 128      127          1
 192      195         -3
 256      259         -3
 320      323         -3
 384      393         -9
 448      454         -6
 512      519         -7
 576      584         -8
 640      650        -10
 704      713         -9
 768      778        -10
 832      842        -10
 896      909        -13
 960      973        -13
>
```

Figure 41 AD conversion results

From Figure 41, we can see that the conversion error increases for higher duties to a maximum of -13 bit. This value is equal to a voltage of (-13/1024) * 3.3 V = 41.89 mV. I inspected the analog input with an oscilloscope and could see higher frequent noise on this line, which is partly due to the breadboard installation.

The quality of an analog signal generated by PWM always depends on the filter used.

If PWM is not a solution to build an analog voltage, then an external digital-to-analog converter (DAC) can be an alternative. In Chapter 6.2.8, I describe a DAC based on Microchip's MCP4725 with a resolution of 12 bit.

6.2.6. DHT11/DHT22

The sensors DHT11 & DHT22 are cost-effective sensors to measure temperature and humidity, which can be integrated into a measuring system very easily.

The following features can be expected from these sensors:

	DHT11	DHT22
Supply Voltage / IO	3 – 5 V DC	
Current consumption max.	2.5 mA	
Humidity	20 – 80% at 5%	0 – 100% at 2–5 %
Temperature	0 – 50 °C at +- 2%	-40 – 125 °C at +- 0.5%
Measuring rate max.	1 / sec	2 / sec
Dimensions	15.5 x 12 x 5.5 mm	15.1 x 25 x 7.7 mm
Pins	4	

The connection of such a sensor to an ESP8266 device goes over three of the four pins. Apart from VCC and GND, a serial data line serves as data interface (Figure 42).

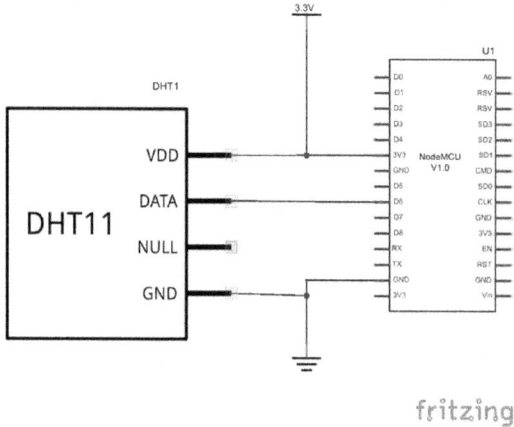

fritzing

Figure 42 DHT11 connected to NodeMCU-devkit

The data interface is proprietary and timing-sensitive. In the program sample *read_DHT11.lua* (Listing 18), the file *dht11.lua* is responsible for the correct timing and the access to the DHT11/DHT22 sensor.

To load and run libraries, Lua offers the higher-level function require(). This function is used here to load the file *dht11.lua* (DHT= require("dht11")). The initialization assigns the pin for data exchange (DHT.init(PIN)). After that, only two function calls are required to read the values of temperature and humidity.

At the end of the program sample, I use the two instructions DHT = nil and package.loaded["dht11"] = nil to remove the unneeded module from memory.

```lua
-- Title   : Read DHT11/DHT22 sensor
-- Author  : Claus Kuehnel
-- Date    : 2015-06-06
-- Id      : read_dht11.lua
-- Firmware: nodemcu_float_0.9.6-dev_20150406
-- Copyright © 2015 Claus Kuehnel info@ckuehnel.ch

PIN = 6 --  data pin to connect DHT11/DHT22

DHT= require("dht11")

DHT.init(PIN)

print("Reading DHT11")

t = DHT.getTemp()
h = DHT.getHumidity()

if h == nil then
  print("Error reading from DHT11/22")
else
  -- temperature in degrees Celsius  and Farenheit
  -- floating point and integer version:
  print("Temperature: "..t.." deg C")
  print("Temperature: "..(9 * temp / 50 + 32).." deg F")

  -- humidity
  print("Humidity: "..h.."%")
end

-- release module
DHT = nil
package.loaded["dht11"]=nil
```

Listing 18 Source code *read_dht11.lua*

Figure 43 shows the call of the program *read_dht11.lua* and the console output of the measured value of temperature and humidity.

```
COM33 - PuTTY
> dofile("read_dht11.lua")
Reading DHT11
Temperature: 27 deg C
Temperature: 36.86 deg F
Humidity: 37%
>
```

Figure 43 Calling program *read_dht11.lua* and result output

6.2.7. 1-Wire

1-Wire designates a serial interface introduced by Dallas Semiconductor. One data line (DQ) is responsible for data exchange and supplies the 1-Wire device with power. However, in any case, a GND line is still required, which is why a minimum of two lines for such an interface is necessary.

Numerous sensors, as also small memory devices, are equipped with the 1-Wire interface. A good overview of 1-Wire components can be found under http://goo.gl/cCgdZp.

A detailed sample program for the use of the temperature sensor DS18B20 can be found in the NodeMCU documentation at the URL https://goo.gl/GGjGxr. For reasons of space, the reference to that source must suffice here.

Figure 44 shows how to connect the DS18B20 to the NodeMCU-devkit. The connection to Pin D9 (RX) is used here to be compatible with the sample program in the documentation mentioned. Basically, each IO pin can be used to connect a 1-Wire device.

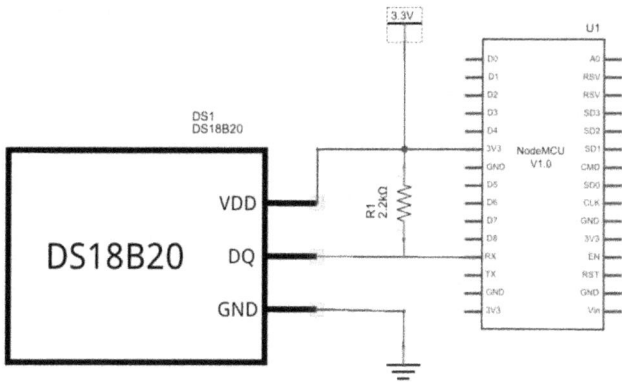

Figure 44 DS18B20 connected to NodeMCU-devkit

6.2.8. I²C Bus

The I²C bus is a serial bus system connecting numerous sensors and/or modules over short distances. It is an advantage that a complete network can be built with just two data lines (SCL, SDA). Additionally, we need VCC and GND.

A fairly comprehensive overview of the various I²C devices can be found at http://goo.gl/Y8lqsz and http://www.i2cdevlib.com/.

In the NodeMCU documentation, there is a program sample that reads the calibration data of a BMP108 sensor (https://goo.gl/vCYugX). This program sample is very good usable as a pattern for own implementation. To save space, here, too, the reference to that source must suffice.

Figure 45 shows how to connect an I²C device to the NodeMCU-devkit. The connection to pin D1 (SDA) and pin D2 (SCL) is used here to be compatible with the sample program in the documentation mentioned. Basically, each IO pin can be used to connect the I²C lines.

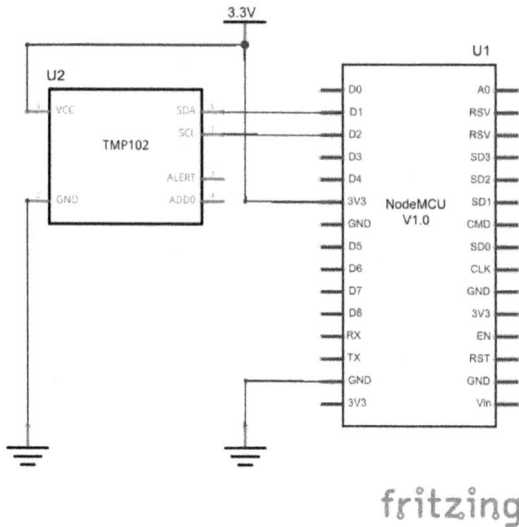

Figure 45 Connecting an I^{2}C device to the NodeMCU-devkit

As a second I^{2}C device, I will connect a MCP4725 Breakout Board (12-Bit DAC) to get a performance enhanced DAC solution compared to the PWM version, introduced in Chapter 6.2.5.

The connection to the NodeMCU-devkit is quite similar (Figure 46). The pull-up resistors needed for the I^{2}C lines are already included in the breakout board. Hence, we can direct connect SDA and SCL. The address line A0 is connected to GND. To connect a second MCP4725, this address line must be connected to VCC for the second device. The output voltage range is 0 to 3.3 V for this circuit.

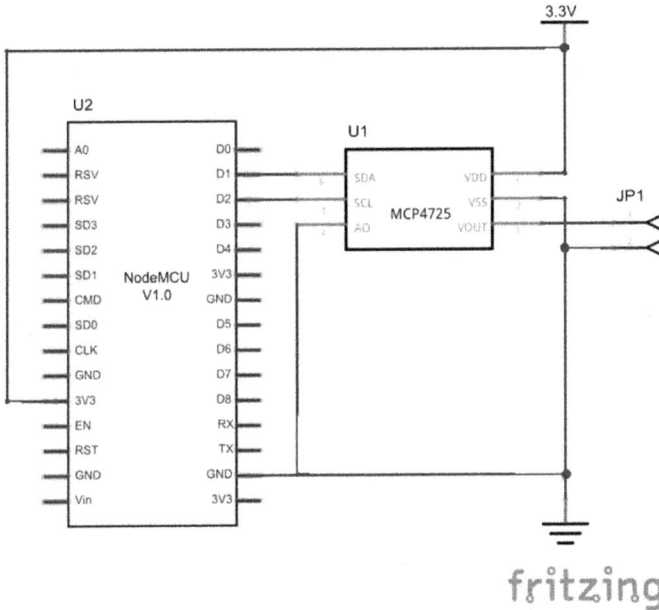

Figure 46 Connecting the MCP4625 Breakout Board to the NodeMCU-devkit

Before we start to code a program sample for I^{2}C devices, it is important to check whether or not they are properly connected. The program *i2c_scan1.lua* helps us answer this question (Listing 19).

At the beginning of the program, some constants for the I^{2}C bus were defined. As already mentioned, we connect SDA to Pin D1 and SCL to Pin D2.

The function `find_dev()` looks for a connected I^{2}C device by evaluating the responded ACK/NACK. If a device with the requested address is connected to the I^{2}C bus, then the function will return true (ACK), otherwise false (NACK). The return value of the function `find_dev()` controls the following print-outs.

```
-- Based on work by sancho and zeroday among many other open
source authors
-- This code is public domain, attribution to
gareth@l0l.org.uk appreciated.
-- Modifications info@ckuehnel.ch 2015-10-10

ID  = 0   -- there is only this one I2C bus
SDA = 1
```

```
SCL = 2

gpio_pin= {5,4,0,2,14,12,13} -- this array maps internal IO
references to GPIO numbers

-- user defined function: see if device responds with ACK to i2c
start
function find_dev(ID, dev_addr)
  i2c.start(ID)
  c=i2c.address(ID, dev_addr ,i2c.TRANSMITTER)
  i2c.stop(ID)
  return c
end

print("Scanning for I2C Bus device")
print("SDA connected to D"..SDA)
print("SCL connected to D"..SCL)
i2c.setup(ID,SDA,SCL,i2c.SLOW)
for i=0,127 do -- TODO - skip invalid addresses
  if find_dev(id, i)== true and i ~= 0 then
    print("\nDevice found at address
0x"..string.format("%02X",i))
    print("Device is wired: SDA to GPIO"..gpio_pin[SDA].." -
IO index "..SDA)
    print("Device is wired: SCL to GPIO"..gpio_pin[SCL].." -
IO index "..SCL)
  end
end
print("\nScan finished.")
```
Listing 19 Source code _i2c_scan1.lua_

We have connected the MCP4725 breakout board with A0 on GND to the NodeMCU-devkit. Running the program i2c_scan1.lua will show an output in accordance with Figure 47. As expected, an I^2C device with the device address 0x62 is connected to the defined SDA and SCL lines. Depending on the logic level at pin A0, the I^2C device address can be 0x62 or 0x63 for an MCP4725.

```
> dofile('i2c_scan1.lua')
Scanning for I2C Bus device
SDA connected to D1
SCL connected to D2

Device found at address 0x62
Device is wired: SDA to GPIO5 - IO index 1
Device is wired: SCL to GPIO4 - IO index 2

Scan finished.
```

Figure 47 Connected I²C Device detected

To test the now available 12-bit DAC, I connect the DAC output to A0 (TOUT) of the NodeMCU-devkit, similar to the PWM example in Chapter 6.2.5.

Listing 20 shows the program *mcp4725.lua*. The function put_DAC() contains some I²C commands, to write a value into the DAC input register.

First, it is checked whether or not the value is in the permitted range from 0 to 4095. If the value exceeds the permitted range, it will be limited to the range.

Then the I²C data exchange is prepared with starting it (i2c.start(ID)), followed by the device addressing for a write operation (i2c.address(ID, MCP4725 ,i2c.TRANSMITTER)). Now, the data bytes follow in accordance with the definitions in the next table.

Command Byte								Data Byte #1								Data Byte #2							
C2	C1	C0	X	X	PD1	PD0	X	D11	D10	D9	D8	D7	D6	D5	D4	D3	D2	D1	D0	X	X	X	X
0	1	0	0	0	0	0	0	value / 16								value % 16 << 4							

The command byte (0x40) defines loading of the configuration bits and data code into the DAC Input Register. The 12-bit data value must be adapted to both the data bytes in the format above.

After writing these three bytes to the MCP4725, the I²C connection is closed (i2c.stop(ID)).

The last section of this program prints the results of the data output sequence (Figure 48).

```lua
ID  = 0
SDA = 1
SCL = 2

MCP4725 = 0x62 -- A0 connected to VSS (GND)
-- MCP4725 = 0c63 -- A0 connected to VDD

CMD = 0x40
STEP = 256

-- initialize i2c, set pin1 as sda, set pin2 as scl
i2c.setup(ID, SDA, SCL, i2c.SLOW)

-- Write value to MCP4725 DAC Input Register
function put_DAC(value)
   if value < 0 then value = 0 end
   if value >= 4096 then value = 4095 end
   i2c.start(ID)
   i2c.address(ID, MCP4725 ,i2c.TRANSMITTER)
   c = i2c.write(ID,CMD, value/16, bit.lshift(value % 16, 4))
   i2c.stop(ID)
   return c
end

print("Reading DAC Output by internal ADC\n")
print("DAC \tADC \tDAC/4-ADC \tdV")
print("=================================")
for value = 0, 4095, STEP do
   put_DAC(value)
   tmr.delay(10 * 1000) -- wait 10 ms to settle
   analog = adc.read(0)
   voltage = (value/4 - analog) * 3300 / 1024
   print(string.format("%4d\t%4d\t%4d\t%6.1f mV",value/4,
analog, value/4 - analog, voltage))
end
```
Listing 20 Source code *mcp4725.lua*

```
> dofile("mcp4725.lua");
Reading DAC Output by internal ADC

DAC     ADC     DAC/4-ADC    dV
=================================
   0       0           0     0.0 mV
  64      62           2     6.4 mV
 128     126           2     6.4 mV
 192     193          -1    -3.2 mV
 256     260          -4   -12.9 mV
 320     326          -6   -19.3 mV
 384     393          -9   -29.0 mV
 448     458         -10   -32.2 mV
 512     523         -11   -35.4 mV
 576     587         -11   -35.4 mV
 640     656         -16   -51.6 mV
 704     720         -16   -51.6 mV
 768     786         -18   -58.0 mV
 832     849         -17   -54.8 mV
 896     918         -22   -70.9 mV
 960     983         -23   -74.1 mV
```

Figure 48 MCP4725 Test Results

I did not expect the deviations that resulted in this test. However, it should be noted that the building of the circuitry, working in a range of millivolts on a bread board, is not optimal.

The results of both options are compared in the DA-AD characteristic shown in Figure 49. Both versions show the same behavior with varying degrees. Therefore, the ESP8266 ADC cannot be ignored, and should be separately evaluated with the right measuring equipment. The information in the ESP8266 data sheet is very rare to this point.

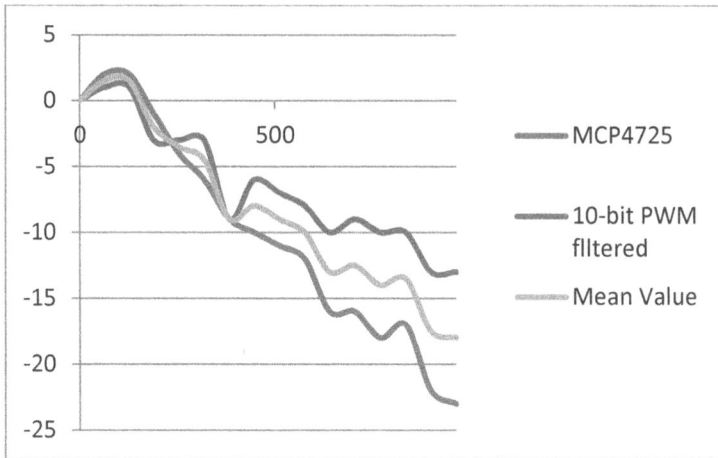

Figure 49 DA-AD Characteristic

6.2.9. OLED Display

Sometimes, it can be very helpful to enhance an IoT node with a small alpha-numeric or graphic display to show states, results, etc. A lot of OLED displays is available. If one googles for that, one will get offers not only from the well-known US vendors, but also from Asians—especially for very low prices.

From eBay, I bought an I^{2}C OLED display with 128 x 64 pixel b&w controlled by an SSD1306 controller for about US $ 10 (Figure 50).

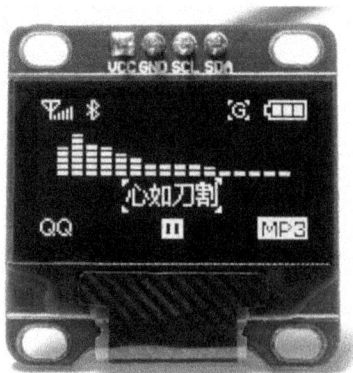

Figure 50 I^{2}C OLED 128x64

The SSD1306 is a single-chip CMOS OLED/PLED driver with controller for organic/polymer light-emitting diode dot-matrix graphic display system. This type of controller is supported by NodeMCU. Further controllers are in the development branch today (https://goo.gl/pRbS5f).

We connect the OLED display to the NodeMCU-devkit, as described in the last chapter (Figure 51). The switch S1 is responsible here for switching between Central European Summer Time (CEST) and Central European Time (CET). CET is 1 hour ahead of Coordinated Universal Time (UTC). If one has in one's area of the world such a Daylight Saving Time, then one can use this switch.

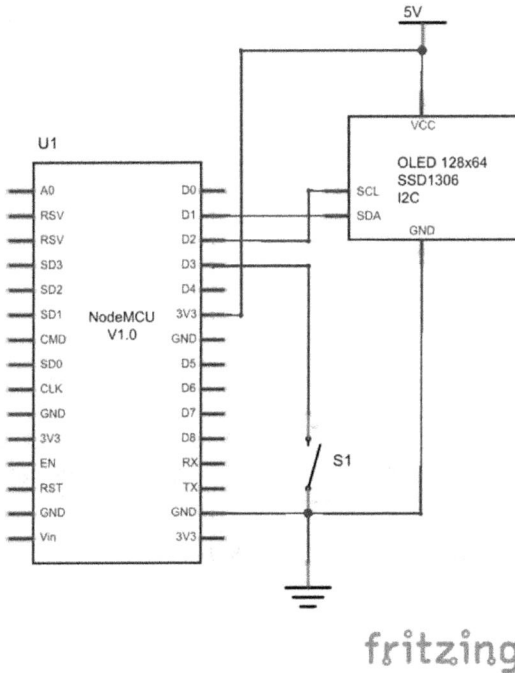

Figure 51 Connecting an I^{2}C OLED 128x64 to the NodeMCU-devkit

To check the function of the I^{2}C bus connection, one can use the program *i2c_scan1.lua* again.

Running this program will show a further I^{2}C bus device with the device address 0x3C connected to the NodeMCU-devkit now, provided that the DAC has not been removed from the bus (Figure 52).

```
dofile('i2c_scan1.lua')
Scanning for I2C Bus device
SDA connected to D1
SCL connected to D2

Device found at address 0x3C
Device is wired: SDA to GPIO5 - IO index 1
Device is wired: SCL to GPIO4 - IO index 2

Device found at address 0x62
Device is wired: SDA to GPIO5 - IO index 1
Device is wired: SCL to GPIO4 - IO index 2
```

Figure 52 New I^{2}C Device detected

I have used the OLED display to show the time queried from Google server by the program *getDateTime.lua*. Listing 21 shows the required modification to control the OLED display in the source code of the program *showtime.lua*.

The function `init_i2c_display()` is important, as it defines the IO pins used for the I^{2}C bus, the device address 0x3C for the SSD1306 controller, and initializes that.

The function `prepare()` initializes several settings, most importantly the font and the scale to be used.

The library U8glib (Universal Graphics Library for 8 Bit Embedded Systems) offers a lot of fonts. Not all of them are available in the standard compilation of NodeMCU.

A look at the file *nodemcu-firmware/app/include/u8g_config.h* shows us that the fonts 6×10 and `chikita` are available here.

```
// Configure U8glib fonts
// add a U8G_FONT_TABLE_ENTRY for each font you want to compile into the
image
#define U8G_FONT_TABLE_ENTRY(font)
#define U8G_FONT_TABLE \
        U8G_FONT_TABLE_ENTRY(font_6x10) \
        U8G_FONT_TABLE_ENTRY(font_chikita)
#undef U8G_FONT_TABLE_ENTRY
```

If one wants to use other fonts, one would have to include them in this configuration file and recompile the whole project.

92

Recompiling the firmware needs a SDK. Not every NodeMCU user will have installed one.

If one wants to build custom NodeMCU firmware for an ESP8266 device, one should build it by the configurable service already introduced in Chapter 4.7 (http://frightanic.com/nodemcu-custom-build/).

One can configure the user modules to also include the desired fonts. Furthermore, one will get a visual impression for each selectable font. We will use this later.

U8glib requires a special programming construct, called "picture loop". The full picture of the graphics device is drawn by looping through the picture loop. In this program sample, the function `printTime()` implements the picture loop.

It usually makes sense to place the graphics commands into their own function. In this program sample, the function `draw()` takes this part. More information on the picture loop is described at https://goo.gl/wcrnlk.

Finally, the function `queryTime()` must be enhanced by calling the picture loop. At the end of the function, I included the call `printTime()` (marked bold), the OLED displays and the queried time as shown in Figure 53.

```lua
-- Title    : Show Google Time on OLED
-- Date     : 2015-10-10
-- Id       : showTime.lua
-- Firmware: nodemcu_float_0.9.6-dev_20150406
-- Modified: Claus Kuehnel

-- setup I2c and connect display
function init_i2c_display()
   -- SDA and SCL can be assigned freely to available GPIOs
   local sda = 1 -- GPIO5
   local scl = 2 -- GPIO4
   local sla = 0x3c
   i2c.setup(0, sda, scl, i2c.SLOW)
   disp = u8g.ssd1306_128x64_i2c(sla)
end

function prepare()
   disp:setFont(u8g.font_6x10)
   disp:setScale2x2()
   disp:setFontRefHeightExtendedText()
   disp:setDefaultForegroundColor()
```

```
  disp:setFontPosTop()
end

-- the draw() routine
function draw()
  prepare()
  string = hour..":"..min
  disp:drawStr(15, 10, string)
end

function printTime()
  disp:firstPage()
  repeat
    draw()
  until disp:nextPage() == false
  tmr.delay(50000)
  tmr.wdclr()  -- re-trigger Watchdog!
end

function queryTime()
  conn=net.createConnection(net.TCP, 0)

  conn:on("connection",function(conn, payload)
  conn:send("HEAD / HTTP/1.1\r\n"..
            "Host: google.com\r\n"..
            "Accept: */*\r\n"..
            "User-Agent: Mozilla/4.0 (compatible; esp8266
Lua;)"..
            "\r\n\r\n")
            end)
  conn:on("receive", function(conn, payload)
    date = string.sub(payload,string.find(payload,"Date: ")
           +6,string.find(payload,"Date: ")+35)
    wday = string.sub(date, 1, 3)
    day = string.sub(date, 6, 7)
    month = string.sub(date, 9, 11)
    year = string.sub(date, 13, 16)
    hour = string.sub(date, 18,19)
    min = string.sub(date, 21, 22)
    sec = string.sub(date, 24,26)
    print(payload)
    print("\n"..day..". "..month..
"..year.."\t"..hour..":"..min..":"..sec.." GMT")
    hour = tostring((tonumber(hour) + 2) % 24)
    hour = "0"..hour
    hour = string.sub(hour, -2)
    print(day..". "..month..
"..year.."\t"..hour..":"..min..":"..sec.." CEST")
    printTime()
    conn:close()
```

```
   end)
  conn:connect(80,'google.com')
end

init_i2c_display()
queryTime()

tmr.alarm(0, 10 * 1000, 1, function() queryTime() end )

print("Queries every 30 sec the time from Google server and
displays it on OLED display")
print("Stop this by tmr.stop(0)")
```

Listing 21 Source code *showtime.lua*

Figure 53 Time Display (Font 6x10)

To make the display more readable, I scaled the used font 6x10 by the scale factor 2x2. If one uncomments this line, one can see the font in the original size.

The result of the scaling is not only a bigger font, but also a roughly pixeled representation of the figures.

To improve the presentation, we can choose another font with a bigger size, but this means changing the firmware.

As already mentioned, we can build a custom NodeMCU firmware using the configurable service http://frightanic.com/nodemcu-custom-build/.

I have included here the font helvR24. Please see Chapter 8.2 for the fonts I have used for the OLED display here.

95

The firmware I built starts with the message shown in Figure 54 and is saved on SourceForge, too.

```
NodeMCU custom build by frightanic.com
    branch: dev096
    commit: e4f79508e1d086a46f90bdf3b9b450e13c3aa015
    SSL: false
    modules: node,file,gpio,wifi,net,i2c,tmr,u8g
    built on: 2015-10-28 17:10
powered by Lua 5.1.4
```

Figure 54 NodeMCU Firmware—Custom Build

To use the bigger font for the time display, a few modifications in the functions prepare() and draw() are only required. Listing 22 shows the modifications marked in bold. The whole file is saved as *showtime1.lua*.

```
function prepare()
  disp:setFont(u8g.font_helvR24)
--  disp:setScale2x2()
  disp:setFontRefHeightExtendedText()
  disp:setDefaultForegroundColor()
  disp:setFontPosTop()
end

-- the draw() routine
function draw()
  prepare()
  string = hour..":"..min
  disp:drawStr(20, 25, string)
end
```

Listing 22 Source code snippet *showtime1.lua*

Figure 55 shows the changed display content and it is significantly more readable with this enhanced font, as the scaled 6x10.

Figure 55 Time Display (Font helvR24)

6.2.10. WS2812 RGB LEDs

A WS2812 device is a combination of a control circuit WS2811 and a RGB LED chip building a serial controlled RGB LED. There are different packages for these devices.

Figure 56 shows a WS2812 RGB LED in a conventional 8mm LED package, while Figure 57 shows it in a 5050 package (5.0 x 5.0 mm^2). In Adafruit's parlance, these devices are named NeoPixel. The 5050 package is very suited for building LED chains or matrixes.

Figure 57
WS2812 RGB LED in 5050 package

Figure 56   WS2812 RGB LED 8 mm

Owing to its serial interface, the WS2812 devices can be cascaded nearly endlessly because the data signal is refreshed from pixel to pixel (Figure 58).

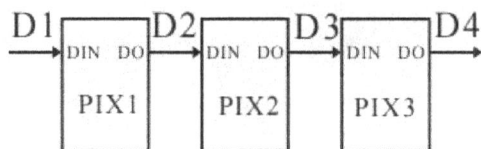

Figure 58 WS2812 Cascading

After the pixel power-on reset, the DIN port receives data from the controller. The first pixel collects initial 24 bit data and sends it to the internal data latch; the other data which is reshaped by the internal signal reshaping amplification circuit is sent through the DO port to the next pixel's DIN in the cascade. After data transmission for each pixel, the data is reduced of 24 bit for the next pixel.

The transmission time for one bit is about 1.25 µs (TH + TL = 1.25 µs ± 600 ns) and the reset time between two refreshes is about 50 µs. Figure 59 shows the timing for the WS2812.

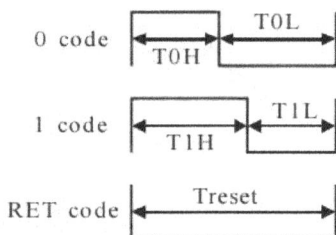

Figure 59 WS2812 Timing

Under these conditions, the refresh rate is defined as

$$f_R = \frac{1}{(24 * T_{bit} * n_{PIXEL}) + T_{reset}}$$

98

and we get a refresh rate of 1887 Hz theoretically.

Owing to the serial connection of Neopixels connecting these to a NodeMCU device, it is independent of their number. It does not matter if we connect one WS2812 RGB LED 8 mm or a NeoPixel Ring - 16 x WS2812 5050 RGB LED (https://goo.gl/w7tUOw) for the hardware implementation, as Figure 60 shows.

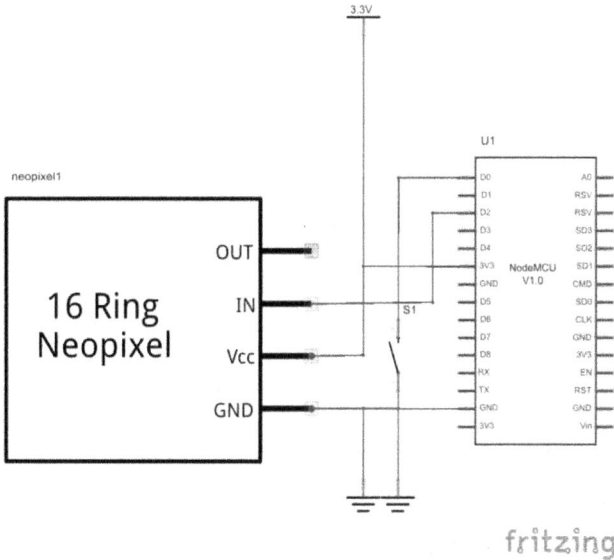

Figure 60 Connecting Neopixel to NodeMCU-devkit

If we connect Pin IN of a WS2812 8 mm RGB LED to the Pin D2 of a NodeMCU device, then we can use a simple program to control the color change of that LED (Listing 23). The push button connected to Pin D0 is not used in this program sample.

To send data to a WS2812 device, NodeMCU offers the command ws2812.writergb(pin, data). To switch all LEDs on a WiFiPixels device to blue, we can use the command ws2812.writergb(4, string.char(0, 0, 255)).

```
-- Date    : 2015-09-24
-- Id      : Wifipixel
-- Firmware: nodemcu_float_0.9.6-dev_20150704
-- Created : Claus Kuehnel
```

99

```
BRIGHT      = 0.5
ON          = BRIGHT * 255
LED_PIN     = 2         -- GPIO2
TIME        = 500000   -- 0.500 second,  2 Hz

RED   = string.char(ON,  0,  0)
GREEN = string.char( 0, ON,  0)
BLUE  = string.char( 0,  0, ON)
WHITE = string.char(ON, ON, ON)
BLACK = string.char( 0,  0,  0)

function show()
  ws2812.write(LED_PIN, RED)
  tmr.delay(TIME)
  ws2812.write(LED_PIN, GREEN)
  tmr.delay(TIME)
  ws2812.write(LED_PIN, BLUE)
  tmr.delay(TIME)
  ws2812.write(LED_PIN, WHITE)
  tmr.delay(TIME)
  ws2812.write(LED_PIN, BLACK)
end

--show()
tmr.alarm(0, 3000, 1, function() show() end )

print("One WS2812 connected to Pin2 will changes its color
repeatedly")
print("Stop this by tmr.stop(0)")
```
Listing 23 Source code *wifipixel.lua*

The program itself is quite simple. The colors are defined by three bytes each. For RED, for example, only the red channel will get an entry. Its value controls the brightness of this LED. The variable ON sets the brightness to half of the maximum here (RED = string.char(ON, 0, 0) with ON = 127)).

For GREEN and BLUE, it is the same procedure. WHITE is mixed by all colors with the same brightness and BLACK is all LEDs switched off. The function show() contains a sequence of different colors separated by a delay, defining it is on time (tmr.delay(TIME)).

A timer is responsible to call the function show() each 3 seconds.

Listing 24 shows a more complex program sample for a WiFiPixels RGB LED ring with 16 cascaded WS2812 RGB LEDs, as described in Chapter 2.2.8.

Here, Pin D0 is used as an input with pull-up resistor (gpio.mode(BUTTON_PIN, gpio.INPUT, gpio.PULLUP)).

After the start of the program, the whole ring blinks with the color sequence, as in the program sample earlier.

Following that a timer calls periodically the function rainbow() as long as the push-button is pressed. A Lo input level at Pin D0 stops the timer.

```
-- Date    : 2015-09-24
-- Id      : Wifipixels
-- Firmware: nodemcu_float_0.9.6-dev_20150704
-- Found at:
https://github.com/geekscape/nodemcu_esp8266/blob/master/exa
mples/ws2812.lua
-- Copyright (c) 2015 by Geekscape Pty. Ltd.  Licence LGPL
V3.
-- Modified: Claus Kuehnel

BRIGHT      = 0.1
ON          = BRIGHT * 255
BUTTON_PIN = 0         -- GPIO0
LED_PIN    = 2         -- GPIO2
PIXELS     = 16        -- WifiPixels have 16 adressable LEDs
on-board
TIME_ALARM = 25        -- 0.025 second, 40 Hz
TIME_SLOW  = 500000    -- 0.500 second,  2 Hz

RED   = string.char(ON,  0,  0)
GREEN = string.char( 0, ON,  0)
BLUE  = string.char( 0,  0, ON)
WHITE = string.char(ON, ON, ON)
BLACK = string.char( 0,  0,  0)

gpio.mode(BUTTON_PIN, gpio.INPUT, gpio.PULLUP)

function colourWheel(index)
   if index < 85 then
      return string.char(index * 3 * BRIGHT, (255 - index * 3)
* BRIGHT, 0)
   elseif index < 170 then
      index = index - 85
      return string.char((255 - index * 3) * BRIGHT, 0, index
* 3 * BRIGHT)
   else
      index = index - 170
      return string.char(0, index * 3 * BRIGHT, (255 - index *
```

```lua
3) * BRIGHT)
  end
end

rainbow_speed = 8

function rainbow(index)
  buffer = ""
  for pixel = 0, PIXELS - 1 do
    buffer = buffer .. colourWheel((index + pixel *
rainbow_speed) % 256)
  end
  return buffer
end

if true then
  ws2812.write(LED_PIN, RED:rep(PIXELS))
  tmr.delay(TIME_SLOW)
  ws2812.write(LED_PIN, GREEN:rep(PIXELS))
  tmr.delay(TIME_SLOW)
  ws2812.write(LED_PIN, BLUE:rep(PIXELS))
  tmr.delay(TIME_SLOW)
  ws2812.write(LED_PIN, WHITE:rep(PIXELS))
  tmr.delay(TIME_SLOW)
  ws2812.write(LED_PIN, BLACK:rep(PIXELS))
end

rainbow_index = 0

function rainbowHandler()
  if gpio.read(BUTTON_PIN) == 1 then
    ws2812.write(LED_PIN, rainbow(rainbow_index))
    rainbow_index = (rainbow_index + 1) % 256
  else
    tmr.stop(1)
    print("rainbowHandler: EXIT");
  end
end

tmr.alarm(1, TIME_ALARM, 1, rainbowHandler)
```

Listing 24 Source code *wifipixels.lua*

6.3. Web Server

In an IoT node, one would hardly want to evaluate outputs from the console, but instead want to access these wirelessly. Using a Web server, the recorded data can be made available to the outside world. NodeMCU offers for that an appropriate interface.

We want to continue recording temperature and humidity, but make this available for display through a request from a Web browser. Listing 25 shows the source code of the program *dht11_webserver.lua*.

A LED is connected to Pin D8 to signalize the access by the Web browser with a short light pulse.

Following the function `readDHT11()`, there is the actual web server, which separates the event "receive" in the received command from the total payload. When a message is received, several printouts then follow. At last, we find a commented-out print of the entire payload for later analysis.

In the string `reply_begin`, the first part of the website to be displayed is built before the actual command from the payload is decoded. The payload begins with the characters `GET /DHT11 HTTP/1.1`, said to be decoded command is `DHT11`.

If the command `DHT11` was found at the expected position, then the rest of the site can be created and finally sent back to the browser.

The event "sent" then also provides for closing the connection, after all.

```
-- Title   : DHT11 Webserver
-- Author  : Claus Kuehnel
-- Date    : 2015-06-06
-- Id      : dht11_webserver.lua
-- Firmware: nodemcu_float_0.9.6-dev_20150406
-- Copyright © 2015 Claus Kuehnel info[at]ckuehnel.ch

PIN = 6 -- data pin of DHT11
LED = 8 -- D8

gpio.mode(LED, gpio.OUTPUT)

DHT= require("dht11")
DHT.init(PIN)

function readDHT11()
  DHT= require("dht11")
```

```lua
  DHT.init(PIN)
  gpio.write(LED,gpio.LOW)
  t = DHT.getTemp()
  h = DHT.getHumidity()
  if h == nil then
    error = 1
    print("Error reading from DHT11")
  else
    error = 0
    print("Temperature: "..t.." deg C\tHumidity:
"..h.."%\n\n")
  end
  gpio.write(LED,gpio.HIGH)
  DHT = nil
  package.loaded["dht11"]=nil
end

-- LUA Webserver --
srv=net.createServer(net.TCP)
srv:listen(80,function(conn)
  conn:on("receive",function(conn,payload)
    print("Got query...")
    print("Heap = "..node.heap().." Bytes")
    print("Time since start = "..tmr.time().." sec")
    -- print("Print payload:\n"..payload)

    reply_begin = "<html><head><title>DHT11 ESP8266
Webserver</title>
</head><body><h1>DHT11 Measuring Values</h1><font
size=\"+2\">"

    -- 123456789012
    -- GET /DHT11 HTTP/1.1 --
    command = string.sub(payload, 6,10) -- Get characters 6
to 10
    if (command == "DHT11") then
      readDHT11()
      reply = reply_begin.."Temperature: "..t.." deg C<br>"
      reply = reply.."Humidity: "..h.."%"
      reply = reply.."</font></body></html>"
    else
      reply = reply_begin.."No access to data."
      reply = reply.."</font></body></html>"
    end
    payloadLen = string.len(reply)
    conn:send("HTTP/1.1 200 OK\r\n")
    conn:send("Content-Length:" .. tostring(payloadLen) ..
"\r\n")
    conn:send("Connection:close\r\n\r\n")
    conn:send(reply)
```

```
    collectgarbage()
    end)

  conn:on("sent",function(conn)
    conn:close()
    end)
end)
```
Listing 25 Source code *dht11_webserver.lua*

Figure 61 shows the call by the web browser. The IoT nodes here have the IP 192.168.1.16, so the call must happen in the form `192.168.1.16/DHT11`. Based on the displayed image in the web browser, one can very well find the relationship with the source code. An extension of the display is easy possible.

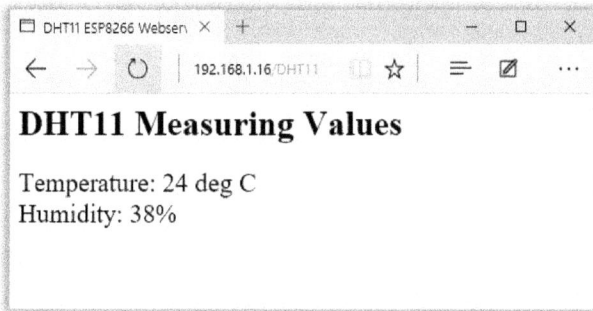

Figure 61 Requesting Temperature and Humidity

6.4. Data Exchange via dweet.io

Dweet.io implemented a publishing-subscribing mechanism for machines, sensors, embedded systems, robotics, etc. Dweet.io referred published messages as "dweets" and sees itself as a "Twitter for things".

A "thing" is a unique name assigned, and a subscriber can subscribe to the related messages.

6.4.1. dweet.io to try

Before we implement the data exchange based on NodeMCU, we want to try the mechanism of data exchange. For this, https://dweet.io/play/ provides an appropriate environment (Figure 62).

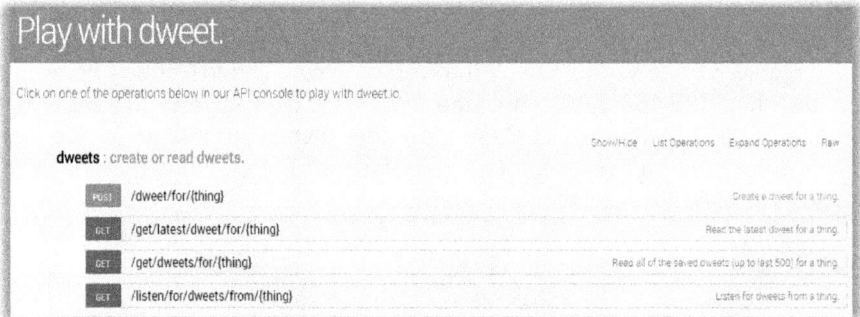

Figure 62 dweet.io playground (detail)

At this point, I want to send a message (publishing) and limit the reception to the last message sent.

For this, the first two commands qualify. To post a message (dweet), the POST command should be used. Figure 63 shows the details.

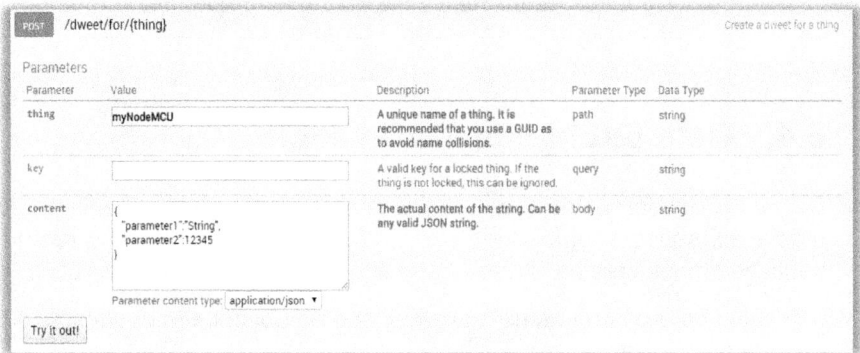

Figure 63 Sending a Dweet

106

The content of a dweet follows the JSON format:

```
{ "parameter1":"String, "parameter2":12345 }
```

Here, these two records were passed. Based on the response, not shown here, the success or failure in sending the dweet is indicated.

The command shown in Figure 64 queries the last sent dweet now. Here, the response is shown after a successful query in a separate listing (Listing 26).

| GET | /get/latest/dweet/for/{thing} | | | Read the latest dweet for a thing |

Parameters

Parameter	Value	Description	Parameter Type	Data Type
thing	myNodeMCU	A unique name of a thing.	path	string
key		A valid key for a locked thing. If the thing is not locked, this can be ignored.	query	string

Try it out!

Figure 64 Query the last sent Dweet

```
{
  "this": "succeeded",
  "by": "getting",
  "the": "dweets",
  "with": [
    {
      "thing": "myNodeMCU",
      "created": "2015-06-24T12:12:30.029Z",
      "content": {
        "{ \"parameter1\":\"String\", \"parameter2\":12345
}": ""
      }
    }
  ]
}
```

Listing 26 Response to the Query for the last sent Dweet

The same operations can also be made independent of the dweet.io playground. Figure 65 shows the sending of a dweet with modified content from a web browser. In the response, the status ("succeeded") and the sent data

107

```
{\"parameter1\":\"Next String\", \"parameter2\":1234567890}
```
are visible.

Figure 65 Sending a Dweet from a Web Browser

Finally, Figure 66 shows the query of the last sent dweet again. In the response, the status ("succeeded") and the data already given can be seen. With reference to the time, the specification ("created": "2015-06-24T12: 23: 07.736Z") is also evident that it is the dweet just sent.

Figure 66 Query the last sent Dweet from Web Browser

6.4.2. NodeMCU as Publisher/Subscriber

An IoT node can assume both the role of a publisher and the role of a subscriber.

A sensor node is a typical representative of a publisher. It sends its messages to the broker, without worrying about their use.

In the program sample, *dweet.lua* (Listing 27), a sensor signal `temp` is simulated by a pseudo-random number. The pseudo-number generator is implemented by the file *random.lua,* which is called by `dofile("random.lua")`. The dweet.io host address is saved in the variable HOST.

The function `dweet()` contains all handling activities with the host.

In addition, the current heap size is transmitted in order to analyze the memory requirements for a long time.

A timer calls every 60 seconds the function `dweet()`, and provides for the sending of data until the timer is stopped by `tmr.stop(0)`.

```
-- Title    : Send data to dweet.io
-- Date     : 2015-07-30
-- Id       : dweet.lua
-- Firmware: nodemcu_float_0.9.6-dev_20150704
-- Created  : Claus Kuehnel

-- Initialize pseudo-random number generator
dofile("random.lua")

HOST = "dweet.io"

function dweet()
  temp = math.random(100)
  conn=net.createConnection(net.TCP,0)
  conn:on("receive", function(conn, pl) print("response:
",pl) end)
  conn:on("connection", function(conn, payload)
          print("connected")
          conn:send("POST /dweet/for/myNodeMCU?"
    .. "temperature=" .. temp
    .. "&heap=" .. node.heap()
    .. " HTTP/1.1\r\n"
    .. "Host: " .. HOST .. "\r\n"
    .. "Connection: close\r\n"
    .. "Accept: */*\r\n\r\n") end)
  conn:on("disconnection", function(conn, payload)
```

```
        print("disconnected") end)
  conn:connect(80, HOST)
end

-- dweets every 60 sec.
tmr.alarm(0, 60 * 1000, 1, function() dweet() end )

print("Dweets every 60 sec a pseudo-random number to
dweet.io")
print("Stop this by tmr.stop(0)")
```

Listing 27 Source code *dweet.lua*

We are now able to follow the activities via dweet.io by calling the last dweet. Figure 67 shows the call in question and the answer. Date and time and the actual content of this announcement

```
   "content" :  { "temperature": 9, "heap":  21072 }
```

show the simulated temperature value and the actual heap size.

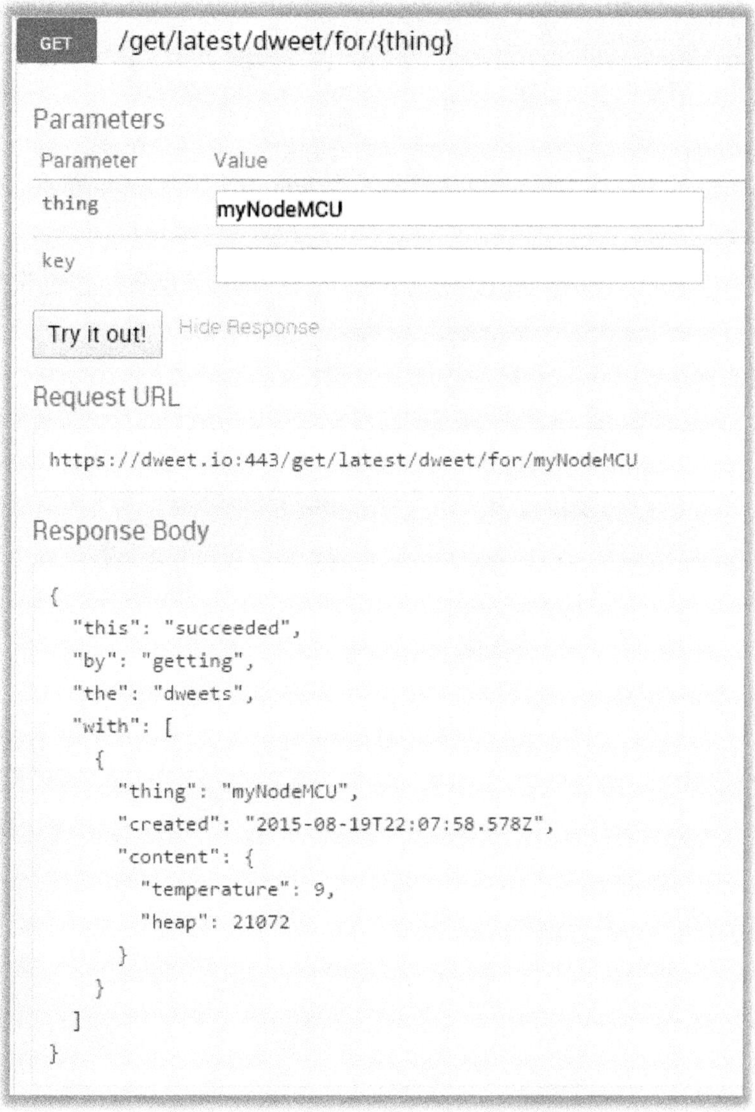

| GET | /get/latest/dweet/for/{thing} |

Parameters

Parameter	Value
thing	**myNodeMCU**
key	

[Try it out!] Hide Response

Request URL

```
https://dweet.io:443/get/latest/dweet/for/myNodeMCU
```

Response Body

```
{
  "this": "succeeded",
  "by": "getting",
  "the": "dweets",
  "with": [
    {
      "thing": "myNodeMCU",
      "created": "2015-08-19T22:07:58.578Z",
      "content": {
        "temperature": 9,
        "heap": 21072
      }
    }
  ]
}
```

Figure 67 Query the last sent Dweet

An actuator node, however, is a typical representative of a subscriber who received present messages transmitted from the broker. Here the broker is to be periodically polled by the actuator nodes for simplicity; otherwise, the free range of dweet.io will leave.

111

In the program sample *get_dweet.lua* (Listing 28), a digital output is switched, depending on a transmitted state.

The query `"GET /get/latest/dweet/for/mySwitch"` asks for the last state of `mySwitch`. The function `printResponse()` analyzes the payload on validity (`200 OK`) and filters the state `{"state":0}` or `{"state":1}`. According to the filtered state, the LED is switched on or off.

Figure 68 shows the output of the payload. To build the function `printPayload()`, it is important to know the formatting of the payload. Otherwise, one cannot disassemble the string defined.

```lua
-- Title    : Asks for latest dweet
-- Date     : 2015-07-30
-- Id       : get_dweet.lua
-- Firmware: nodemcu_float_0.9.6-dev_20150704
-- Created : Claus Kuehnel

HOST = "dweet.io"

LED = 8 -- D8

-- set gpio 0 as output.
gpio.mode(LED, gpio.OUTPUT)
gpio.write(LED, gpio.HIGH)

function printResponse(pl)
  local i = 0
  local j = 0
  print("response: ",pl)
  i = string.find(pl, "200 OK")
  if i ~= nil then
    _, i = string.find(pl, "state")
    state = string.sub(pl, i+3, i+3)
  end
end

function get_last_dweet()
  conn=net.createConnection(net.TCP,0)
  conn:on("receive", function(conn, pl) printResponse(pl)
end)
  conn:on("connection", function(conn, payload)
        print("connected")
        conn:send("GET /get/latest/dweet/for/mySwitch"
        .. " HTTP/1.1\r\n"
        .. "Host: " .. HOST .. "\r\n"
        .. "Connection: close\r\n"
```

```
        .. "Accept: */*\r\n\r\n") end)
  conn:on("disconnection", function(conn, payload)
        print("disconnected")
        gpio.write(LED, state) end)
  conn:connect(80, HOST)
end

-- get_last_dweet()

-- asks for latest dweet every 60 sec. and controls D8
tmr.alarm(0, 60 * 1000, 1, function() get_last_dweet() end )

print("Asks every 60 sec for the latest dweet from
dweet.io")
print("Stop this by tmr.stop(0)")
```

Listing 28 Source code *get_dweet.lua*

Figure 68 Output of the Payload

As Figure 69 shows, I used dweet.io again to specify the desired state.

Parameters

Parameter	Value
thing	mySwitch
key	
content	{"state":0}

Parameter content type: application/json ▼

Try it out!   Hide Response

Request URL

```
https://dweet.io:443/dweet/for/mySwitch
```

Response Body

```json
{
  "this": "succeeded",
  "by": "dweeting",
  "the": "dweet",
  "with": {
    "thing": "mySwitch",
    "created": "2015-08-19T21:47:39.556Z",
    "content": {
      "state": 0
    }
  }
}
```

Figure 69 Posting a Dweet

6.4.3. Visualization with freeboard.io

Data provided by dweet.io can easily be visualized in a dashboard on freeboard.io.

After registration, one can opt for one of the price plans shown in Figure 70. For the tests here, the FREE option is sufficient.

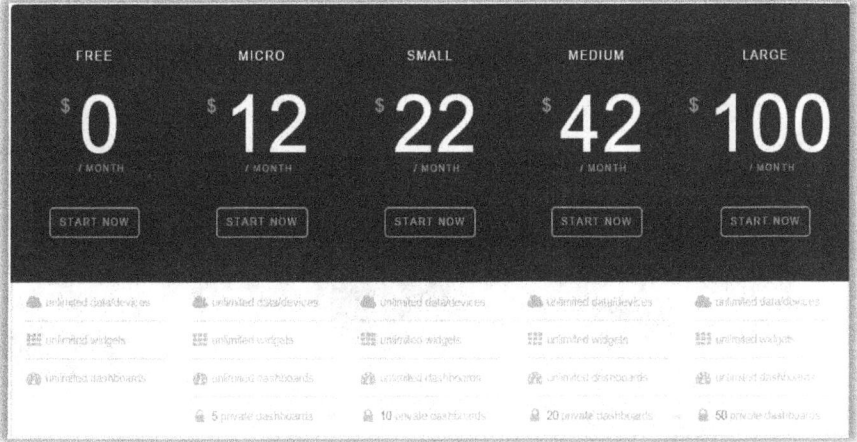

Figure 70 freeboard.io Prices

To create a dashboard, we can use drag & drop and parameterization of the generated fields (Panes).

Figure 71 shows an example of such a dashboard to visualize the transmitted data in the last sample program. The heap data was issued for monitoring, and moves here between 13,384 and 13,376 KBytes.

Figure 72 shows the link to the data stored in dweet.io, which should be displayed in the freeboard.io dashboard.

115

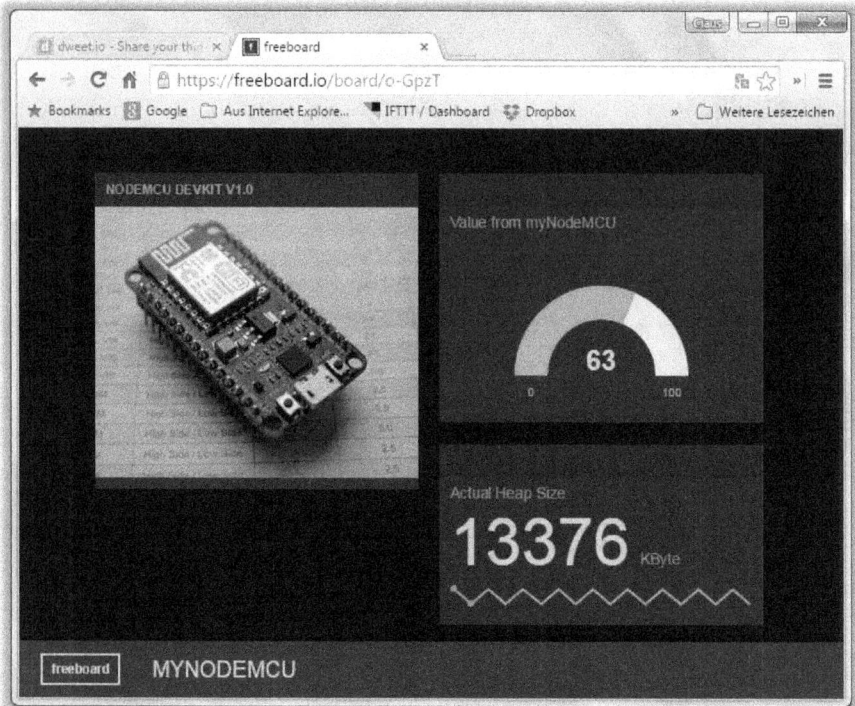

Figure 71 freeboard.io Dashboard

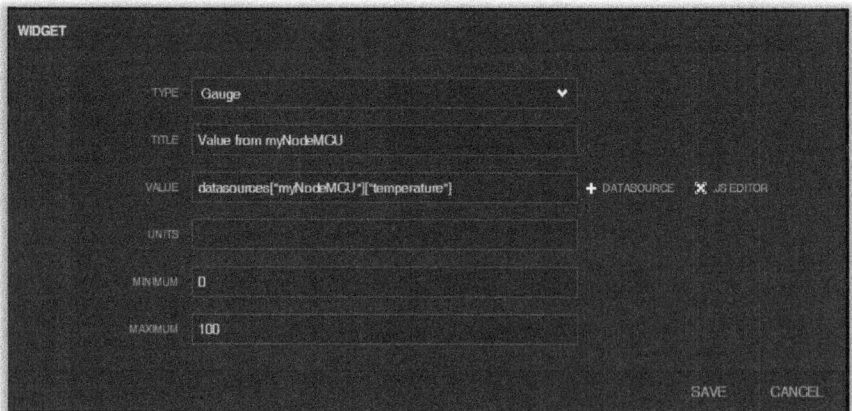

Figure 72 Linking the Data

6.5. MQTT

The protocol Message Queuing Telemetry Transport (MQTT) is an extremely simple built publish-subscribe protocol for exchanging messages between devices with less functionality. The robust MQTT protocol has been developed for unreliable networks with low bandwidth and high latency.

MQTT minimizes the network bandwidth used and the requirements for equipment; at the same time, a high reliability is achieved for the data transmission. These requirements are especially prevalent in sensor networks, in Machine-to-Machine (M2M), telemedicine, patient monitoring and the "Internet of Things". In this application, the connected devices are "Always On" and communicate constantly with each other.

The open, royalty-free MQTT protocol has been developed for satellite communications in 1999 by IBM and later used in many industrial applications. Since 2013 OASIS standardized MQTT as the protocol for the Internet of Things. OASIS is a non-profit consortium that drives the development, convergence and adoption of open standards for the global information society.

The structure, in which the MQTT protocol operates, consists of a data source, which is referred to as a publisher, the data sink, the subscriber and the intermediary message broker that provides the communication controller (https://goo.gl/16hrNn). Figure 73 shows the model in question.

Figure 73 Publish/Subscribe Message Queuing Model

In order to become familiar with the MQTT, the use of a free broker service is offered as a playground. CloudMQTT of the Swedish company 84codes AB is such a possibility.

6.5.1. CloudMQTT

CloudMQTT are Mosquitto servers in the cloud. Mosquitto is an open source Message Broker (BSD license) that implements the MQTT protocol in Versions 3.1 and 3.1.1.

To create a CloudMQTT instance, it is necessary to set up an account under http://www.cloudmqtt.com/ and to opt for a customer plan. There are plans for different customer needs (Figure 74). As a test site, I use the free *Cute Cat*.

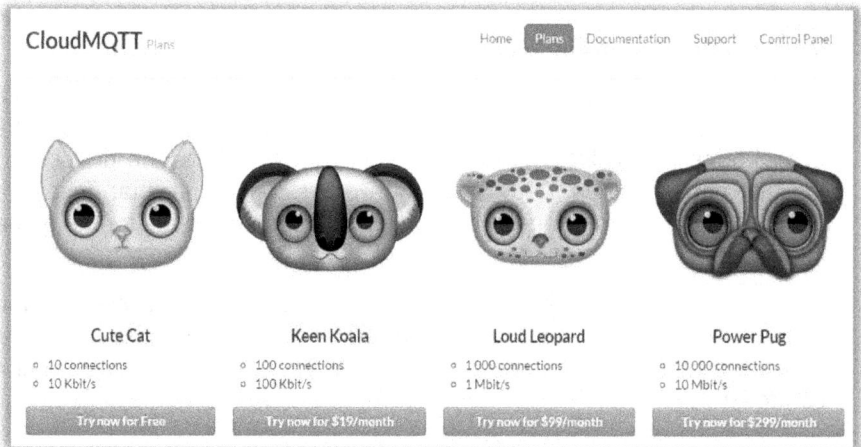

Figure 74 CloudMQTT Plans

The registration of a customer account occurs via an email address to which a link will be sent to unlock it. Figure 75 shows the login in the *Cute Cat* plan.

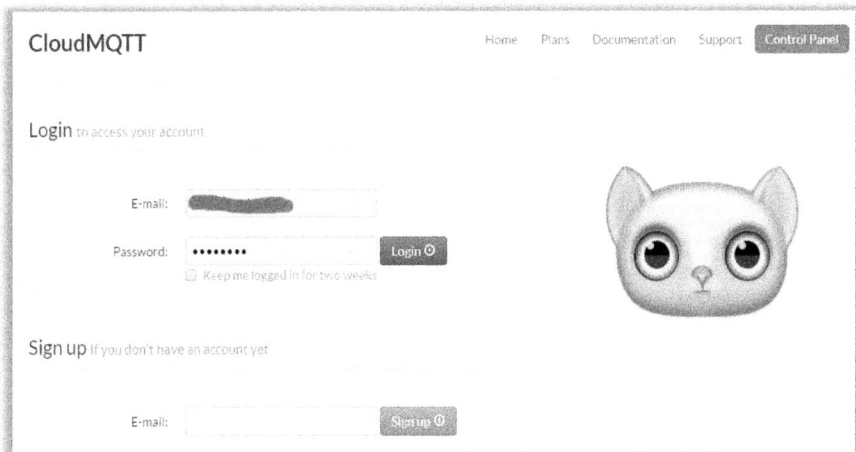

Figure 75 CloudMQTT Login

After creating an instance of CloudMQTT, the information to the generated instance is displayed. All data shown in Figure 76 is assigned by the system. This is also true for the username and password.

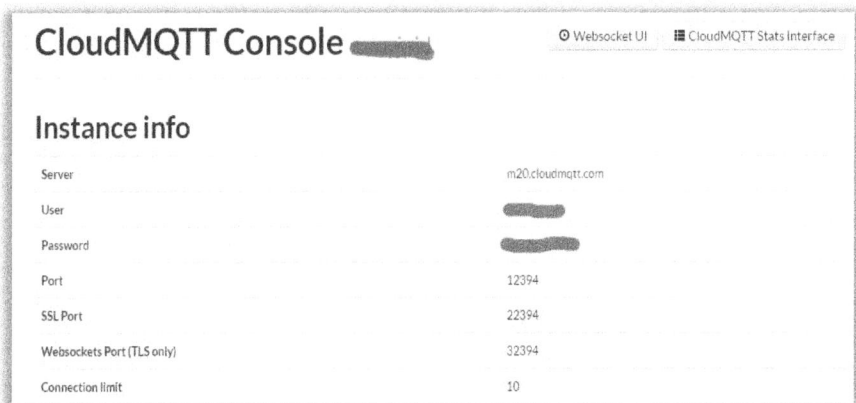

Figure 76 CloudMQTT Instance Info

Before data can be exchanged via the MQTT protocol, the so-called ACL Rules must be defined. ACL stands for Access Control List. I have here the topic `/my/topic`, equipped with read and write permissions (Figure 77).

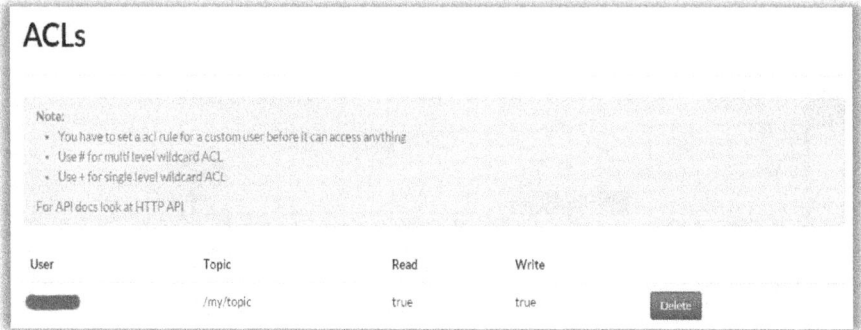

Figure 77 Definition of ACL Rule

In this way, all preparations have been made on the server side, and the data exchange can be tested via the Websocket U(ser) I(nterface). Figure 78 shows sending of messages and logging of receipt.

Figure 78 Test via Websocket User Interface

6.5.2. NodeMCU as MQTT Publisher

As a first step, we want to publish sensor data to the MQTT broker already mentioned. The sensor data will be simulated again by pseudo-random numbers.

For this purpose, we have to load the file *random.lua* at the beginning of the program.

120

The credentials are enhanced by the login data of CloudMQTT, i.e., BROKER, BRPORT, BRUSER, and BRPWD. The client ID (CLIENTID) is built from the Chip ID (CLIENTID = "ESP8266-" .. node.chipid()).

Listing 29 shows the source code of the program *mqtt.lua*.

```
-- Title   : Publish data to cloudmqtt.com
-- Date    : 2015-08-24
-- Id      : mqtt.lua
-- Firmware: nodemcu_float_0.9.6-dev_20150704
-- Found at:
      http://git.agocontrol.com/hari/esp8266-lua-
snippets/blob/master/mqtt.lua
-- Modified: Claus Kuehnel


-- Defined in credentials.lua
-- CLIENTID, BROKER, BRPORT, BRUSER, BRPWD

-- Initialize pseudo-random number generator
dofile("random.lua")

print "Connecting to MQTT broker. Please wait..."

temperature = math.random(100) -- simulates values between 0
and 99
pressure = math.random(100) -- simulates values between 0
and 99

m = mqtt.Client(CLIENTID, 120, BRUSER, BRPWD)

m:connect( BROKER, BRPORT, 0, function(conn)
   print("Connected to MQTT:"..BROKER..":"..BRPORT.." as
"..CLIENTID)

m:publish("/sensors/"..CLIENTID.."/temperature",temperature,
0,0,
    function(conn)
    print ("temperature value published")
    tmr.delay(10000)
```

```
m:publish("/sensors/"..CLIENTID.."/pressure",pressure,0,0,
function(conn)
      print ("pressure value published")
      tmr.delay(10000)
    end)
  end)
end)

m:close()
```
Listing 29 Source code *mqtt.lua*

After the preparations mentioned, the MQTT Client is defined, and publishes two (simulated) sensor data.

Figure 79 shows the console output, while Figure 80 visualizes the sensor data received by MQTT Broker via Websocker UI.

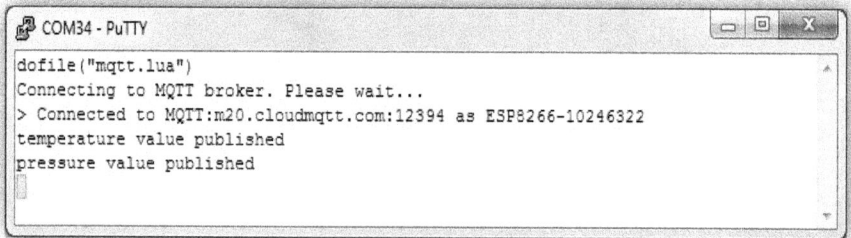

Figure 79 Publishing Sensor Data

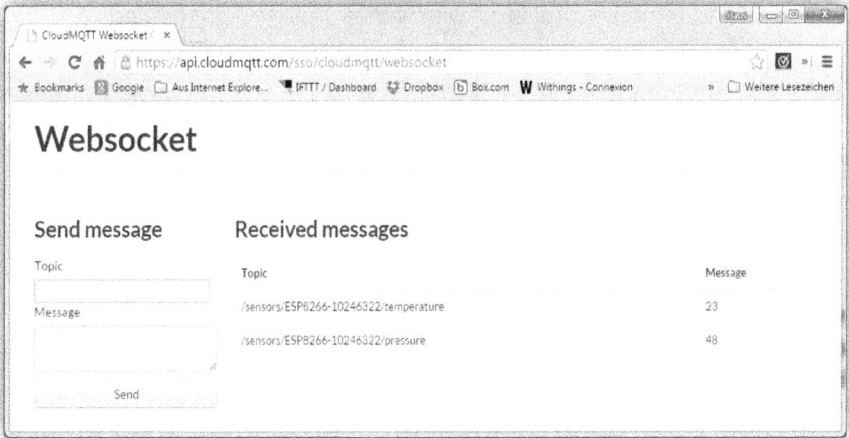

Figure 80 Received Sensor Data by MQTT Broker

6.5.3. Cloud-based Presence Detection

The next program sample will show the combination of publishing and subscribing for a presence detector.

For detection of presence, I use a PIR sensor HC-SR501, as shown in Figure 81. One can find a lot of offers for a small amount of money on the Web and introductions on YouTube, etc.

Figure 81 PIR Detector HC-SR501

For us, it is interesting that it has digital output only. It has a 3.3 V output level and a series resistor of 1 kΩ on its output; thus, no level shifter is needed. A data sheet can be downloaded from https://goo.gl/E9CB6q.

123

One can simply connect the PIR detector output to an IO pin (here Pin D1). Pin D2 controls a LED with series resistor, connected to signalize the PIR state.

The program sample *pir.lua* is the implemention of a MQTT publisher sending a status message to the MQTT broker when the input state at Pin D1 is changing (Listing 30).

After connecting the MQTT client to the MQTT broker, each second the function `read_input(IN)` queries the PIR detector output state. If the state has changed, the LED is switched on or off, and a message is outputted to the console and published to the MQTT broker. This cycle can be stopped by calling `tmr.stop(0)` via console.

```lua
-- Title   : MQTT PIR Sensor
-- Date    : 2015-06-07
-- Id      : pir.lua
-- Firmware: nodemcu_float_0.9.6-dev_20150406
-- Created : Claus Kuehnel info[at]ckuehnel.ch

-- Connect LED & resistor to Pin2 (D2) of NodeMCU
-- Connect PIR Output to Pin1 (D1) of NodeMCU

LED = 2 -- D2
IN  = 1 -- D1

old_state = 1

-- set gpio 2 as output.
gpio.mode(LED, gpio.OUTPUT)

-- CLIENTID = "ESP8266-" .. node.chipid()

print "Connecting to MQTT broker. Please wait..."
-- init mqtt client with keepalive timer 120sec
m = mqtt.Client(CLIENTID, 120, BRUSER, BRPWD)

-- setup Last Will and Testament (optional)
-- Broker will publish a message with:
-- qos = 0, retain = 0, data = "offline"
-- to topic "/lwt" if client don't send keepalive packet
m:lwt("/lwt", "offline", 0, 0)

m:on("connect", function(con) print ("connected") end)
m:on("offline", function(con) print ("offline") end)

-- on publish message receive event
m:on("message", function(conn, topic, data)
```

```
    print(topic .. ":" )
    if data ~= nil then
      print(data)
    end
end)

-- for secure: m:connect("192.168.11.118", 1880, 1)
m:connect(BROKER, BRPORT, 0, function(conn)
    print("Connected to MQTT:"..BROKER..":"..BRPORT.." as
"..CLIENTID)
end)

-- set gpio 1 as input w/ pullup
gpio.mode(IN, gpio.INPUT, gpio.PULLUP)

function read_input(pin)
    state = gpio.read(IN)
    if state ~= old_state then
      old_state = state
      print("PIR State = "..state)
      if state == 1 then
        gpio.write(LED, gpio.LOW)
        m:publish("/pir/"..CLIENTID.."/state",state,0,0,
function(conn) end)
      else
        gpio.write(LED, gpio.HIGH)
        m:publish("/pir/"..CLIENTID.."/state",state,0,0,
function(conn) end)
      end
    end
end

-- input pin is queried every 1000ms
tmr.alarm(0, 1000, 1, function() read_input(IN) end )

print("If input state changes LED connected to Pin8 will
change too")
print("Stop this by tmr.stop(0)")
```

Listing 30 Source code *pir.lua*

Now it is possible to look for the published messages via Websocket UI, as explained in the last chapter. Here, we want to use a second NodeMCU device to subscribe to these messages, and start an action in accordance with the message content.

For the program sample *pir_sub_mqtt.lua,* I use the Olimex ESP8266-EVB with its on-board relay controlling a LED with a little bit more power (Listing 31).

The credentials must be enhanced by the PUBLISHERID. This is the CLIENTID of the publisher. This ID builds the connection between publisher and subscriber.

After connecting the MQTT client to the MQTT broker, the client subscribes to the topic /pir/PUBLISHERID/state. If the published state equals 0, then we will get the message "No further movement" via the console, and the connected relay will be switched off. Otherwise, we will get the message "Movement detected" and the relay will be switched on.

If the MQTT client loses the connection, which is signalized by "offline" then a re-connection is attempted.

```
-- Id       : pir_sub_mqtt.lua
-- Firmware: nodemcu_float_0.9.6-dev_20150704
-- Found at: http://git.agocontrol.com/hari/esp8266-lua-
snippets/blob/master/mqtt.lua
-- Modified: Claus Kuehnel

-- Defined in credentials.lua
-- CLIENTID, BROKER, BRPORT, BRUSER, BRPWD

REL = 1 -- Relay of ESP8266-EVB is connected to GPIO5

-- init mqtt client with keepalive timer 120sec
m = mqtt.Client(CLIENTID, 120, BRUSER, BRPWD)

-- m:on("offline", function(con) print ("offline") end)
m:on("offline", function(con)
     print ("Reconnecting to MQTT:" .. BROKER)
     print("Heap = " .. node.heap())
     tmr.alarm(1, 1000, 0, function()
          m:connect(BROKER, BRPORT, 0)
     end)
end)

m:connect(BROKER, BRPORT, 0, function(conn)
  print("Connected to MQTT:"..BROKER .."":"..BRPORT.." as
"..CLIENTID )
  -- subscribe topic with qos = 0
  m:subscribe("/pir/".. PUBLISHERID .. "/state",0,
  function(conn)
    print("subscribe success")
  end)
  -- on publish message receive event
  m:on("message", function(conn, topic, data)
    if data ~= nil then
```

```
      print(topic..":"..data)
      if data == "0" then
        print("No further movement")
        gpio.write(REL, gpio.LOW)
      else
        print("Movement detected")
        gpio.write(REL, gpio.HIGH)
      end
    end
  end)
end)
```

Listing 31 Source code *pir_sub_mqtt.lua*

6.5.4. MQTT Links

I recommend these specific sites for further information on MQTT for NodeMCU:

- Nodemcu and MQTT: How to start (https://goo.gl/JqD7Wb)
- ESP8266 lua snippets (http://goo.gl/GQQa7u)
- An inexpensive IoT enabler using ESP8266 (http://goo.gl/LNd4CG)

6.6. IFTTT

IFTTT gives one creative control over products and apps, and may be useful for building one's cloud-based applications.

IFTTT stands for "If This Then That", as the following example will show.

6.6.1. IFTTT Maker Channel

IFTTT started off as a way to connect online tools and services, triggering one from the other. For instance, one can have a "recipe," as IFTTT tasks are called, that automatically takes every new photo one posts on Instagram and saves it to one's Dropbox. If this: one posts a photo. Then that: save it to Dropbox (http://goo.gl/vO1tao).

Later, it will be possible that "connected home" products, like Nest Thermostat, SmartThings, WeMo switches, and Wink devices, can receive and/or send data.

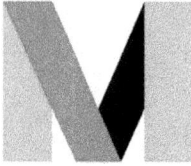

Now, the Maker Channel allows one to connect IFTTT to one's personal DIY projects. With Maker, one can connect a recipe to any device or service that can make or receive a web request.

One can see a lot of projects using the IFTTT Maker channel at <u>hackster.io</u>.

As always, we have to create an IFTTT account to use IFTTT. One need not worry, as it is free.

One has to sign in into IFTTT at first and then one can create recipes. I will explain the use of the Maker channel of IFTTT in the next few chapters.

6.6.2. Creating an IFTTT Recipe

For example, I want to monitor a door contact to see the time at which this door is opened or closed. This door event should trigger a tweet.

As the next step, we have to follow seven steps to define that IFTTT receipt starting with *Create Receipt*.

In a first step, we have to choose a trigger channel. IFTTT offers a lot of different trigger channels; we have to look for the Maker Channel in this case. Typing in "maker" reduces the offered option to Maker and WeMo Maker, and we can select the Maker Channel we have searched for (Figure 82). The Maker Channel offers only one trigger and we have to choose it (Figure 83).

Figure 82 Choose a Trigger Channel

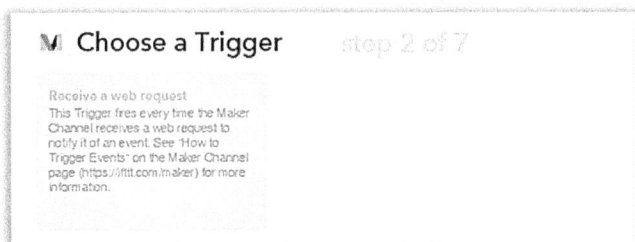
Figure 83 Choose a Trigger

The trigger event must be named; we will do this in the next step. This name will be sent from the NodeMCU device in its request and will build the bridge between our IoT node and IFTTT. As Figure 84 shows, I simply chose the name "door".

Figure 84 Complete Trigger Fields

After pressing *Create Trigger,* Step 3 is finalized, and the IF part is defined now (Figure 85). To go further, we have to click *that* now.

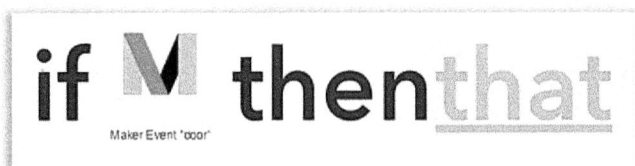
Figure 85 IF part finished

The triggered action must be chosen as the next step. The Action Channel is, in our example, Twitter; after typing the first few letters, Twitter will be offered, and can be selected (Figure 86).

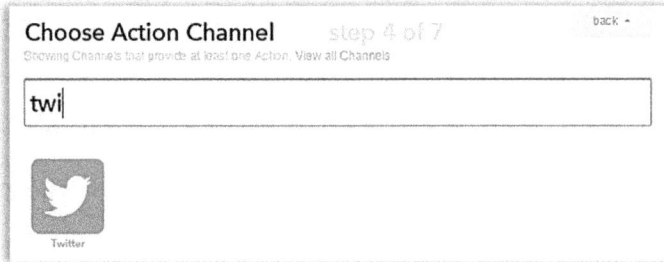

Figure 86 Choose Action Channel

Several actions on Twitter are possible, as Figure 87 shows. I choose "Send a direct message to yourself" because the door movements are interesting only for me.

Direct Messages comprise the private side of Twitter. One can use Direct Messages to hold private conversations with Twitter users about Tweets and other content.

The message in Figure 88 itself is the default message. We can change it later; we press *Create Action* now.

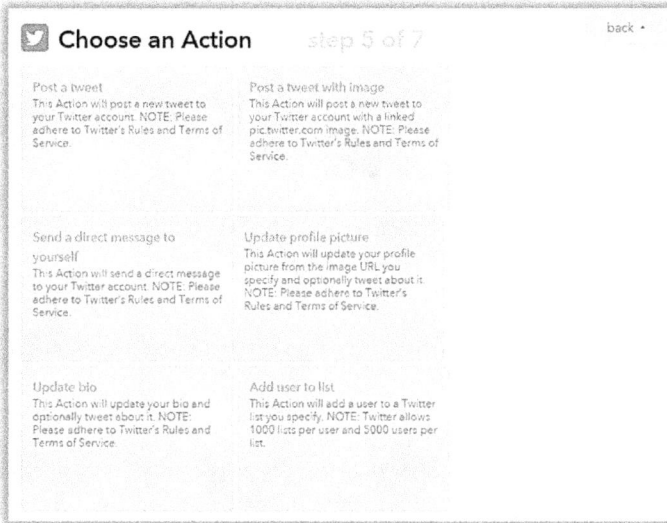

Figure 87 Choose an Action

Figure 88 Complete Action Fields

Now the last step of this procedure will follow; we can give a meaningful recipe title. I let the default title remain unchanged for this test. Pressing *Create Recipe* finalizes this process (Figure 89).

Figure 89 Create and connect

We can now find the created Maker recipe as the last recipe at *MyRecipes* (Figure 90) and can edit it at any time.

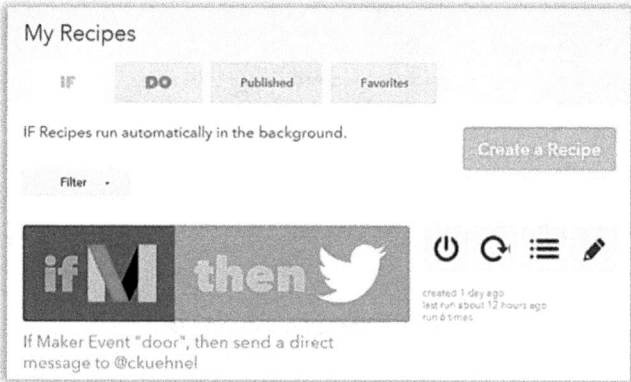

Figure 90 Added Recipe

As Figure 91 shows, I change the tweet text, which was not changed in Step 6. Up to three variables can be sent from the IoT node within the tweet message. Here `value1` is used, enhanced by `OccurredAt`, containing the date and time information of the event. Pressing Update will finally save the changes in the recipe.

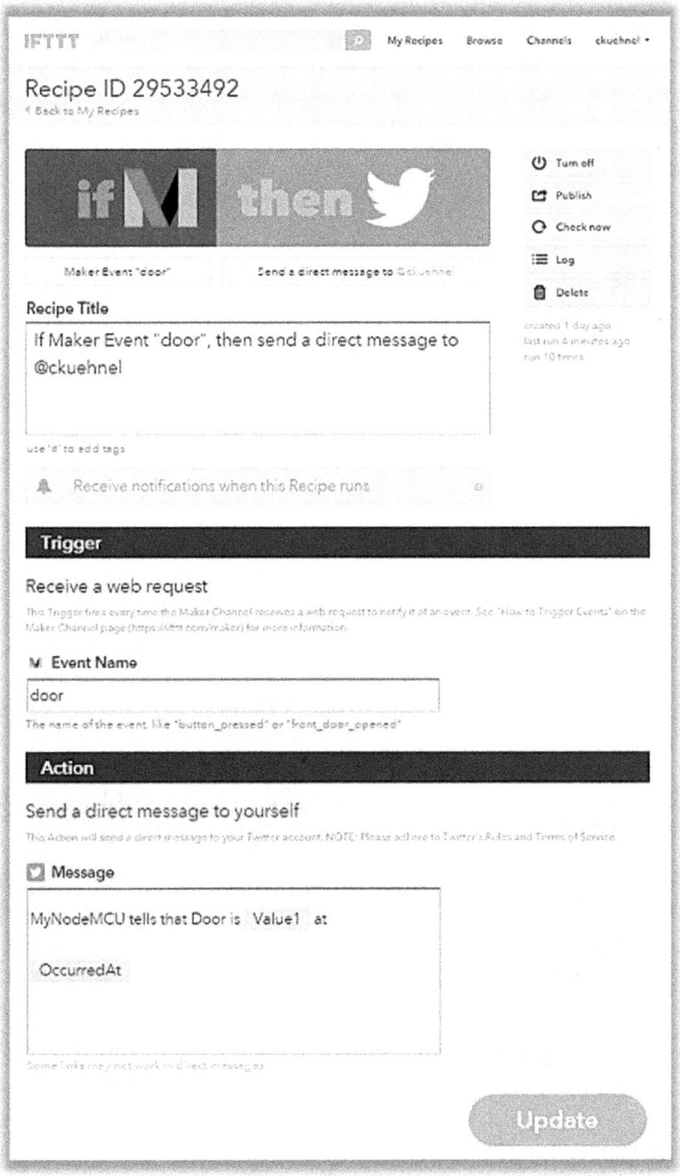

Figure 91 Updating a Maker Recipe

The created Maker recipe is now ready for use; we have to implement the program on the IoT node that generates the trigger event for this recipe.

6.6.3. Door Contact Monitoring

To monitor the movement of a door or window, we can use door contacts, as shown in Figure 92. On the top part, a Reed contact is installed, which will be closed when the lower part containing a permanent magnet comes near to the Reed contact.

If the door or window is closed, then both parts are close to each other and the Reed contact is normally closed. Otherwise, the Reed contact will be open, and signalizes an open door or window.

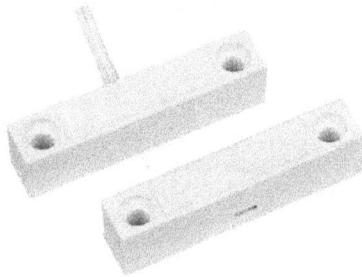

Figure 92 Door Contact

In the program sample *ifttt.lua* (Listing32), such a contact is monitored each second by calling the function `read_input()`.

If the state of the input changes, then the new input state is printed to the console. The on-board LED on the NodeMCU-devkit, connected to Pin D0, is switched on when the contact connected to Pin D4 is closed. Otherwise, the LED is switched off. At the beginning of the program, the IOs are defined and initialized.

The part of the program responsible for the connection to IFTTT is the function `sendData()`. This function builds an TCP client which connects to IFTTT (`conn:connect(80,'maker.ifttt.com')`) and sends a POST request to the IFTTT Maker Channel (`conn:send("POST /trigger/`**door**`/with/key/"..`**IFTTTKEY**`.."?value1="..state.`

." HTTP/1.1\r\n...")). The POST request contains the event "door" and the IFTTTKEY, which comes from the IFTTT account.

The IFTTTKEY is separated from the application file *ifttt.lua* and saved in the file *credentials.lua*.

All other events print their states to the console. The state which should be transferred is added in the POST request by "?value1=".. state.

```lua
-- Title   : IFTTT
-- Author  : Claus Kuehnel
-- Date    : 2015-10-30
-- Id      : ifttt.lua
-- Firmware: nodemcu_float_0.9.6-dev_20150406
-- Based on:
-- https://www.hackster.io/fablabeu/first-esp8266-and-ifttt-
integration
-- Guido Burger (http://fab-lab.eu/)

-- IO
LED = 0
IN  = 4

-- set D4 as input w/ pullup
gpio.mode(IN, gpio.INPUT, gpio.PULLUP)

-- set D0 as output
gpio.mode(LED, gpio.OUTPUT)
gpio.write(LED, gpio.LOW)
tmr.delay(100)
gpio.write(LED, gpio.HIGH)

function sendData(state)
  -- conection to IFTTT channel
  print("Sending data to IFTTT channel")
  conn=net.createConnection(net.TCP, 0)
  conn:on("receive", function(conn, payload) print(payload)
end)
  conn:connect(80,'maker.ifttt.com')
  conn:on("connection", function(conn, payload)
    print("Connected, sending event")
    conn:send("POST
/trigger/door/with/key/"..IFTTTKEY.."?value1=".. state.."
HTTP/1.1\r\n")
    conn:send("Host: maker.ifttt.com\r\n")
    conn:send("Accept: */*\r\n")
    conn:send("User-Agent: Mozilla/4.0 (compatible; esp8266
Lua; Windows NT 5.)\r\n")
    conn:send("\r\n")
```

```
  end)

  conn:on("sent",function(conn)
    print("Closing connection")
    conn:close()
  end)

  conn:on("disconnection", function(conn)
    print("Got disconnection...")
  end)
end

function read_input(pin)
  state = gpio.read(pin)
  if state ~= old_state then
    old_state = state
    print("Input = "..state)
    if state == 0 then
      gpio.write(LED, gpio.LOW)
      sendData("closed")
    else
      gpio.write(LED, gpio.HIGH)
      sendData("opened")
    end
  end
end

read_input(IN)

-- input pin is queried every 1000ms
tmr.alarm(0, 1000, 1, function() read_input(IN) end )

print("If input state changes LED connected to D0 will
change too")
print("Stop this by tmr.stop(0)")
```
Listing 32 Source code *ifttt.lua*

Figure 93 shows the console output of the running program *ifttt.lua* for changing input states. This output can easily be compared with the source code.

136

```
Input = 0
Sending data to IFTTT channel
Connected, sending event
Closing connection
Got disconnection...
Input = 1
Sending data to IFTTT channel
Connected, sending event
Closing connection
Got disconnection...
```

Figure 93 Console output *ifttt.lua*

Something more of interest are the received tweets. I made a screenshot of four tweets from my mobile phone (Figure 94). Comparing this output to the defined message in Figure 91, the transferred parameter value1 has two states, either "opened" or "closed", followed by the date and time information.

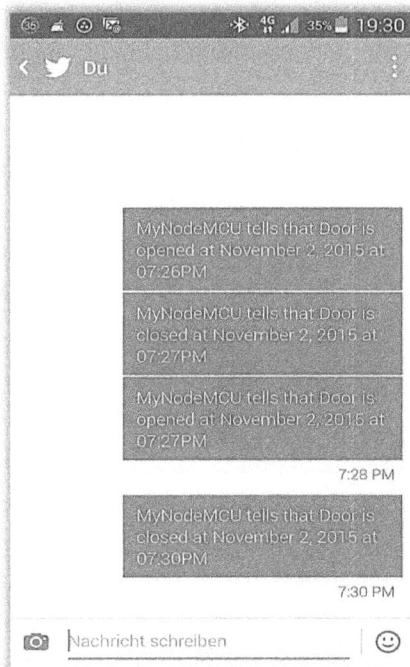

Figure 94 Received Door Status

6.7. Benchmarks

A benchmark should be a quantitative test that measures something meaningful, delivers correct results, and produces similar results when repeated in similar circumstances (http://goo.gl/LKvCul).

The benchmarks introduced in the following chapters can be used to compare NodeMCU devices with other Lua-based IoT nodes. With NodeMCU and WifiMCU, we have two systems programmable in Lua, but equipped with different microcontrollers and WLAN devices. The results of the benchmark for both controllers are shown in my WiFiMCU Gitbook (https://goo.gl/1ybiXB)

6.7.1. Sieve of Erastosthenes

The Sieve of Eratosthenes is one of the most efficient ways to find all of the smaller primes and is a well-known CPU benchmark.

Listing 33 shows the program *bm1.lua*, an implementation of the Sieve of Eratosthenes with global variables. The program *bm2.lua* works with local variables for x and iter. This is the only difference. The file *bm2.lua* is available for download from Sourceforge, but not listed here.

```
function sieve(n)
  x = {}
  iter = 0
  repeat
    x[1] = 0
    i = 2
    repeat
      x[i] = 1
      i = i + 1
    until i > n
    p = 2
    while(p * p <= n) do
      j = p
      while(j <= n) do
        x[j] = 0
        j = j + p
      end
      repeat
        p = p + 1
      until x[p] == 1
    end
```

```
    iter = iter + 1
  until iter == 101
end

print("Sieve of Eratosthenes - Lua Benchmark")
print("=======================================")
print("Start testing …..")
start = tmr.now()
sieve(500)
stop = tmr.now(0)
print("Done!")
print("Total Time = " .. (stop - start)/1000 .. " ms")
```

Listing 33 Source code *bm1.lua*

The results of both benchmarks are listed in Figure 95. The compiled versions, *bm1.lc* and *bm2.lc,* show the same runtime behavior.

```
> dofile("bm1.lua");
Sieve of Eratosthenes - Lua Benchmark (Global Variables)
=======================================================
Start testing .....
Done!
Total Time = 2756.869 ms
> dofile('bm2.lua')
Sieve of Eratosthenes - Lua Benchmark (Local Variables)
=======================================================
Start testing .....
Done!
Total Time = 1057.489 ms
```

Figure 95 Sieve of Eratosthenes—Benchmark Results

6.7.2. *Factorial*

The calculation of the factorial is another well-known simple CPU benchmark. Factorial is defined for a positive integer as

$$n! = n * (n - 1) \ldots 2 * 1$$

So, for example, 4! = 4 * 3 * 2 * 1 = 24.

Listing 34 shows the source code of the file *FactorBench.lua.* The program calculates the value of 20! = 2.4329020081766e+18. The accuracy of the result can be verified by an online calculation, for

139

example. Please take a look at http://goo.gl/ZTvNjC for that. The resulting runtime of this benchmark is shown in Figure 96.

```
-----------------------------------------------------------------
-- CPU Benchmark
-----------------------------------------------------------------

CYCLES = 1000

function factorial(n)
   local x = 1.
   for i = 2,n do
     x = x * i
   end
   return x
end


x=20 print("Calculating fak("..x..") as benchmark")

local t = tmr.now()   -- due to quick access defined as local

-----------------------------------------------------------------
-- Benchmark runtime of code phragments
-----------------------------------------------------------------
for n=1, CYCLES do factorial(x) end --user code
-----------------------------------------------------------------

print("For "..CYCLES.." cycles of calculation")
print("fak("..x..") = "..factorial(x))
print("Elapsed time: "..string.format("%.3f",(tmr.now() -
t)/1000).." ms")
```

Listing 34 Source code *FactorBench.lua*

```
dofile('FactorBench.lua')
Calculating fak(20) as benchmark
For 1000 cycles of calculation
fak(20) = 2.4329020081766e+18
Elapsed time: 148.486 ms
```

Figure 96 FactorBench—Benchmark Results

6.7.3. IOBench

For bit-banging operations, it is very important to know the possible speed of switching an IO pin. Therefore, I have added the program *IOBench.lua* to these benchmarks. The program itself is quite simple.

For a defined number of cycles (here `CYCLES` = `1000`), the Pin D8 is switched on and off. From the runtime of the loop and the number of cycles, an output frequency is calculated.

Listing 35 shows the source code of the program *IOBench.lua* and Figure 97 the results of this benchmark.

```
---------------------------------------------------------
-- IO Bench Mark
---------------------------------------------------------

CYCLES = 1000

-- Connect LED & resistor to Pin8 (D8) of NodeMCU
LED = 8 -- D8

-- set gpio 8 as output.
gpio.mode(LED, gpio.OUTPUT)

-- get start time
local t = tmr.now() -- us

---------------------------------------------------------
-- Benchmark runtime of code phragments
---------------------------------------------------------
for i = 1, CYCLES do
  gpio.write(LED, gpio.LOW)
  gpio.write(LED, gpio.HIGH)
end
---------------------------------------------------------

t = tmr.now() - t
print("IO Cycle    = "..t/CYCLES.." us")
print("IO Frequency = ".. string.format("%.2f",
1000*CYCLES/t).." kHz")
```
Listing 35 Source code *IOBench.lua*

```
> dofile('IOBench.lua')
IO Cycle     = 537.786 us
IO Frequency = 1.86 kHz
```

Figure 97 IOBench—Benchmark Results

It is possible to speed up the digital output by replacing gpio.write() with gpio_write (gpio_write = gpio.write), as demonstrated in Chapter 6.2.3. The IO frequency then rises to 3.3 kHz.

6.8. Reduction of power consumption

To reduce the power consumption of the NodeMCU, we can set the module to sleep mode between actions.

For an IoT node, it is possible to query a sensor and go into sleep mode until the next query comes. The power consumption will be reduced by the ratio between the duration of normal operation and sleep mode.

For the resulting current consumption, we get the following equation:

$$\bar{I} = \frac{I_{OP} * t_{OP} + I_{SLEEP} * t_{SLEEP}}{t_{OP} + t_{SLEEP}}$$

The index OP marks the values for normal operation while the index SLEEP marks the values during sleep mode.

If we have a current consumption of about 65 mA for an operational time of 5 sec and go into sleep afterward for 60 s with a measured current consumption of 108 µA, then we will get a mean value of about 5 mA. A sleep period of 120 s would reduce the mean value of current consumption to 2.7 mA.

For 5 mA current consumption, we can expect the following lifetimes for different types of batteries:

Battery Type	Capacity	Lifetime	
CR1212	18 mAh	3.6 h	0.15 d
CR1620	68 mAh	13.6 h	0.57 d
CR2032	210 mAh	42 h	1.75 d
NiMH AAA	900 mAh	180 h	7.50 d
Alkaline AAA	1250 mAh	250 h	10.42 d
NiMH AA	2400 mAh	480 h	20.00 d
Alkaline AA	2890 mAh	578 h	24.08 d
Li-Ion *	4400 mAh	880 h	36.67 d

Table 4 Lifetime calculations for different types of batteries
* Li-Ion batteries come in a wide variety of sizes; this is just an example.

As deep sleep resets the NodeMCU on wakeup, and as we also want our code to start automatically on power up, we have to modify the file *init.lua*. The file is called *myfile.lua*, but a timer is set up. This gives us five seconds to interrupt the "autostart", which is quite helpful during development (or to change SSID settings).

Listing 36 shows the modified source code of *init.lua* and Listing 37 the source of *myfile.lua*.

The program *myfile.lua* calls the application and sets the deep sleep mode after finishing the application. The application called here is the file *nodemcu_info.lua* and serves as an example only. One should not forget to connect pin D0 (GPIO16) with RST to restart NodeMCU after the deep sleep period.

```
--load credentials
--SID and PassWord should be saved according wireless router in use
dofile("credentials.lua")

function startup()
  if file.open("init.lua") == nil then
    print("init.lua deleted")
  else
    print("Running")
    file.close("init.lua")
    dofile("myfile.lua")
  end
end

--init.lua
```

143

```
wifi.sta.disconnect()
print("set up wifi mode")
wifi.setmode(wifi.STATION)
wifi.sta.config(SSID,PASSWORD,0)
wifi.sta.connect()
tmr.alarm(1, 1000, 1, function()
  if wifi.sta.getip()== nil then
    print("IP unavailable, Waiting...")
  else
    tmr.stop(1)
    print("Config done, IP is "..wifi.sta.getip())
    print("You have 5 seconds to abort Startup")
    print("Waiting...")
    tmr.alarm(0,5000,0,startup)
  end
end)
```

Listing 36 Source code of modified file *init.lua*


```
print("Running myfile.lua....")
dofile("nodemcu_info.lua")
print("Going to sleep for 60 sec...")
node.dsleep(60000000) -- sleep 60 sec, D0 (GPIO16) connected to
RST
```

Listing 37 Source code *myfile.lua*

Figure 98 shows an excerpt from the console output for the test of the sleep mode.

144

```
NodeMCU running 8.750737 sec from last restart

Going to sleep for 60 sec... áÈ¤lìÉãhÈ$ølã CñÈ¶i¤h:ìt  ,¤¤f_YütCá
NodeMCU 0.9.6 build 20150704  powered by Lua 5.1.4
set up wifi mode
> IP unavaiable, Waiting...
Config done, IP is 192.168.178.43
You have 5 seconds to abort Startup
Waiting...
Running
Running myfile.lua....
NodeMCU Version 0.9.6

ChipID 10554992
FlashID 1458415 Flashsize 4.096 MByte
Flashmode 2 Flashspeed 40 MHz

File system info:
Total : 3396281 Bytes
Used : 24096 Bytes
Remain: 3372185 Bytes

Remaining heap size is: 25328
NodeMCU running 8.749561 sec from last restart

Going to sleep for 60 sec... á
```

Figure 98 Testing Sleep Mode

The whole procedure starts with the output of

`NodeMCU 0.9.6 build 20150704  powered by Lua 5.1.4`

After connecting to the access point, the program waits five seconds for aborting. If no abort occurs, then the program calls the file *myfile.lua* visible by the output `Running myfile.lua…` followed by the output of the file called `nodemcu_info.lua`. The last action of `myfile.lua` is to call the command `node.dssleep()` to set the deep sleep mode for the NodeMCU.

7.   Conclusion

The idea behind this book was to show that an IoT node can be implemented with few components at low cost. Modules based on the ESP8266 require no further microcontrollers for this purpose.

With NodeMCU, a comfortable Lua development environment is available, which can and complete demanding tasks with only a few lines of code.

Whether Lua will be the language of the "Internet of Things" remains to be seen. For further information, one can read "Lua as a common language for the IoT" (http://www.lua.org/wshop14/Riesberg.pdf). That the use of Lua is very advantageous here could be shown with numerous programming examples.

8.   Appendix

8.1.   GPIO Map

From NodeMCU Build 20141219, the following relationship between the IO index and the ESP8266 Pins is applicable:

IO Index	ESP8266 Pin	IO Index	ESP8266 Pin
0 [*]	GPIO16	7	GPIO13
1	GPIO5	8	GPIO15
2	GPIO4	9	GPIO3
3	GPIO0	10	GPIO1
4	GPIO2	11	GPIO9
5	GPIO14	12	GPIO10
6	GPIO12		

[*] D0 (GPIO16) can only be used as digital IO. Interrupts, PWM, I^2C and 1-Wire are not supported.

8.2.   Used Fonts

The NodeMCU standard firmware offers two fonts for use in graphical representation of ASCII characters on graphic display, like an OLED display.

Figure 99 and Figure 100 show both the standard fonts 6x10 and chikita suitable for multi-line representation on small display (e.g. 128x64).

Figure 101 shows the font u8g_font_helvR24 that I used for the time display to show five characters only on the whole display.

147

```
u8g_font_6x10, X11 Display Font
BBX Width 6, Height 10,  Capital A 7
Font data size: 1866
  32/0x20    ! " # $ % & ' ( ) * + , - . /
  48/0x30    0 1 2 3 4 5 6 7 8 9 : ; < = > ?
  64/0x40    @ A B C D E F G H I J K L M N O
  80/0x50    P Q R S T U V W X Y Z [ \ ] ^ _
  96/0x60    ` a b c d e f g h i j k l m n o
 112/0x70    p q r s t u v w x y z { | } ~
 128/0x80
 144/0x90
 160/0xa0    ¡ ¢ £ ¤ ¥ ¦ § ¨ © ª « ¬ - ® ¯
 176/0xb0    ° ± ² ³ ´ µ ¶ · ¸ ¹ º » ¼ ½ ¾ ¿
 192/0xc0    À Á Â Ã Ä Å Æ Ç È É Ê Ë Ì Í Î Ï
 208/0xd0    Ð Ñ Ò Ó Ô Õ Ö × Ø Ù Ú Û Ü Ý Þ ß
 224/0xe0    à á â ã ä å æ ç è é ê ë ì í î ï
 240/0xf0    ð ñ ò ó ô õ ö ÷ ø ù ú û ü ý þ ÿ
```

Figure 99 u8g_font_6x10

```
u8g_font_chikita, Chikita
BBX Width 9, Height 10,  Capital A 5
Font data size: 2236
  32/0x20    ! " # $ % & ' ( ) * + , - . /
  48/0x30    0 1 2 3 4 5 6 7 8 9 : ; < = > ?
  64/0x40    @ A B C D E F G H I J K L M N O
  80/0x50    P Q R S T U V W X Y Z [ \ ] ^ _
  96/0x60    ` a b c d e f g h i j k l m n o
 112/0x70    p q r s t u v w x y z { | } ~
 128/0x80
 144/0x90
 160/0xa0    ¡ ¢ £ ¤ ¥ ¦ § ¨ © ª « ¬ - ® ¯
 176/0xb0    ° ± ² ³ ´ µ ¶ · ¸ ¹ º » ¼ ½ ¾ ¿
 192/0xc0    À Á Â Ã Ä Å Æ Ç È É Ê Ë Ì Í Î Ï
 208/0xd0    Ð Ñ Ò Ó Ô Õ Ö × Ø Ù Ú Û Ü Ý Þ ß
 224/0xe0    à á â ã ä å æ ç è é ê ë ì í î ï
 240/0xf0    ð ñ ò ó ô õ ö ÷ ø ù ú û ü ý þ ÿ
```

Figure 100 u8g_font_chikita

148

```
u8g_font_helvR24, helvR24
BBX Width 39, Height 48,  Capital A 25
Font data size: 10931
```

32/0x20　　! " # $ % & ' ( ) * + , - . /

48/0x30　　0 1 2 3 4 5 6 7 8 9 : ; < = > ?

64/0x40　　@ A B C D E F G H I J K L M N O

80/0x50　　P Q R S T U V W X Y Z [\ ] ^ _

96/0x60　　` a b c d e f g h i j k l m n o

112/0x70　　p q r s t u v w x y z { | } ~

128/0x80

144/0x90

160/0xa0　　¡ ¢ £ ¤ ¥ ¦ § ¨ © ª « ¬ - ® ¯

176/0xb0　　° ± ² ³ ´ µ ¶ · ¸ ¹ º » ¼ ½ ¾ ¿

192/0xc0　　À Á Â Ã Ä Å Æ Ç È É Ê Ë Ì Í Î Ï

208/0xd0　　Ð Ñ Ò Ó Ô Õ Ö × Ø Ù Ú Û Ü Ý Þ ß

224/0xe0　　à á â ã ä å æ ç è é ê ë ì í î ï

240/0xf0　　ð ñ ò ó ô õ ö ÷ ø ù ú û ü ý þ ÿ

Figure 101 u8g_font_helvR24

149

8.3. LED Features

We connected LEDs to IO pins to visualize states, etc. The brightness of a LED is controlled by the current through the LED in the forward direction. Depending on the semiconductor material used, the color of the light and the forward voltage differ. Table 5 shows typical values for color/wavelength and forward voltage of LEDs.

Color Sample	Color Name	Typical Wavelength (nm)	Typical Forward Voltage (V)
	Red	640	2.0
	Yellow	585	2.1
	Green	568	2.2
	Blue	470	3.5
	White	n.a.	3.5

Table 5 Typical LED Values for Wavelength & Forward Voltage

If one wishes to go deeper into the subject, one can find a very good LED tutorial at http://goo.gl/hMhn9.

8.4. IoT Node Costs

The title of the book promises an IoT node for less than $ 15.

Here, I will list the costs for the components in building such a node (11/08/2015). In most of the cases, we will find one or the other component in our existing equipment, so that the cost of $ 15 is achievable (Table 6).

Component	Vendor/Distributor	Price
ESP8266 SMT Module – ESP-12	Adafruit	$ 6.95
ESP-ADC DIL18 Modul mit ESP8266EX	In-circuit.de	€ 9,90
ESP8266-EVB	Olimex	€ 9.95
NodeMCU LUA Amica R2	Electrodragon	$ 8.94
Adafruit HUZZAH ESP8266 Breakout	Adafruit	$ 9.95
ESP8266 Thing	Sparkfun	$ 15.95

ESP-WROOM-02	Espressif	$ 5.57
ESP8266 Shield	Sparkfun	$ 14.95
WifiPixels	Protoneer	$ 20.00
USB to TTL Serial Cable - Debug / Console Cable for Raspberry Pi	Adafruit	$ 9.95
Zenotech Home Travel Wall AC Charger USB	Amazon.com	$ 5.49
Riipoo 12W / 2.4A USB Power Adapter	Amazon.com	$ 9.99

Table 6 Cost of an ESP8266 IoT Node

8.5. NodeMCU Base Boards

For most of the experiments I conducted for this book, I used a simple bread board. However, sometimes it is helpful to use a base board, as it can reduce the cabling required.

In this chapter, I would like to introduce some base boards available from several vendors. The links provided here lead to further information and offers.

8.5.1. LoLin Base Board

The LoLin base board and the NodeMCU Base ESP8266 Testing DIY Breadboard Plate are the same board, offered by different vendors. It allows a flexible powering with 1A/5V output switching power on board (Max 24V input).

There are four groups of power on the board:

3V　　3.3 V

5V　　5.0 V (will only work after external power supply is plugged in)

VUSB　the power of USB, usually is 5 V (will only work after is USB plugged in)

Vin　　the power of external power supply, max 24 V DC. Recommended 9 V, 12 V

Figure 102 shows the LoLin base board without NodeMCU.

151

Figure 102 LoLin Base Board

For further information regarding the LoLin base board, please take a look at http://goo.gl/HB1rl3.

8.5.2. oddWires ESP8266 Protoboard with ESP-12E Module

The oddWires ESP8266 Protoboard with an ESP-12E module enables rapid prototyping for an IoT project. This protoboard supports SOIC and SOT-23 components as well as DIP and conventional through-hole components. There are five connections to each pin as well as a further 16 interconnected rows of 5 pins on either side of a standard DIP socket width (http://goo.gl/U1ptnx).

One can power the board via the USB/Serial interface, or one can connect a standard 3.3V bread board power supply.

Figure 103 shows the oddWires ESP8266/NodeMCU Protoboard with a connected bread board power supply module, manufactured by the YwRobot Corporation (http://goo.gl/S1aoZU).

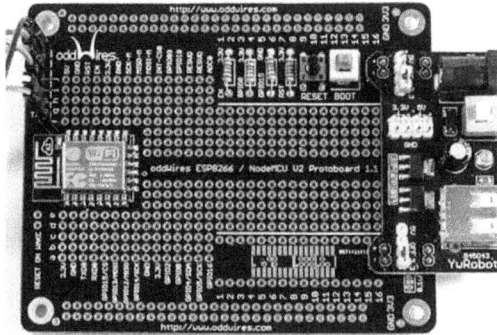

Figure 103 oddWires ESP8266/NodeMCU Protoboard

8.5.3. ESP12-E Motor Drive Shield

A Chinese company, Doctors of Intelligence & Technology (DOIT), designed the ESP-12E Motor Shield. Its ESP12-E Dev Kit is similar to the NodeMCU-devkit v1.0 and higher, and can be plugged into the board directly. Figure 104 shows the ESP12-E Motor Drive Shield without NodeMCU.

This board uses the large power full-bridge chip L293D from STmicroelectronics to drive two DC motors or one stepper motor. A motor current up to 1.2 A can be driven. Further information is available from https://goo.gl/u6YvKt.

Figure 104   ESP12-E Motor Drive Shield

8.5.4. Grove Base Shield for NodeMCU

Grove Base Shield for NodeMCU, offered by Seeed Studio, is an extension board that helps one play with Grove sensors on a NodeMCU-devkit (http://goo.gl/T2sclF).

The Grove Base Shield has the following features:

- Compatible with all Grove modules
- 5 Digital connectors (D3-D8)
- 1 Analog connectors (A0)
- 2 I^2C sockets
- No SPI socket
- UART/D9-D10 connector
- Power indicator LED

Figure 105 shows the Grove Base Shield without NodeMCU.

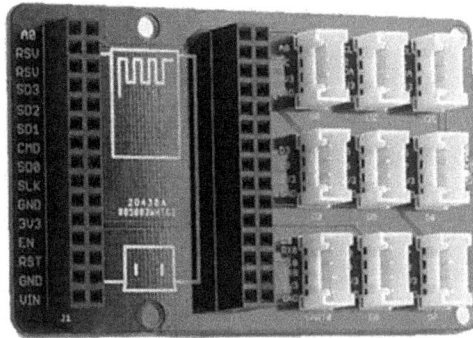

Figure 105 Grove Base Shield for NodeMCU

154

8.6. Licenses

8.6.1. Espressif MIT License

Copyright (c) 2015 <ESPRESSIF SYSTEMS (SHANGHAI) PTE LTD>

Permission is hereby granted for use on ESPRESSIF SYSTEMS ESP8266 only, in which case, it is free of charge, to any person obtaining a copy of this software and associated documentation files (the "Software"), to deal in the Software without restriction, including without limitation the rights to use, copy, modify, merge, publish, distribute, sublicense, and/or sell copies of the Software, and to permit persons to whom the Software is furnished to do so, subject to the following conditions:

The above copyright notice and this permission notice shall be included in all copies or substantial portions of the Software.

THE SOFTWARE IS PROVIDED "AS IS", WITHOUT WARRANTY OF ANY KIND, EXPRESS OR IMPLIED, INCLUDING BUT NOT LIMITED TO THE WARRANTIES OF MERCHANTABILITY, FITNESS FOR A PARTICULAR PURPOSE AND NONINFRINGEMENT. IN NO EVENT SHALL THE AUTHORS OR COPYRIGHT HOLDERS BE LIABLE FOR ANY CLAIM, DAMAGES OR OTHER LIABILITY, WHETHER IN AN ACTION OF CONTRACT, TORT OR OTHERWISE, ARISING FROM, OUT OF OR IN CONNECTION WITH THE SOFTWARE OR THE USE OR OTHER DEALINGS IN THE SOFTWARE.

8.6.2. Arduino Licenses

The main body of the Processing/Arduino code (in general, all the stuff inside the 'app') and 'core' subfolders) is covered by GNU general Public License (GPL). The GNU Lesser general Public License (LGPL) covers the Arduino core and libraries.

To get the complete license texts follow these links:

GPL V2   http://www.gnu.org/licenses/gpl-2.0.html

LGPL V2.1   https://www.gnu.org/licenses/lgpl-2.1.html

8.6.3. NodeMCU License

The NodeMCU firmware is covered by the MIT License.

The MIT License (MIT)

Copyright (c) 2014 zeroday nodemcu.com

Permission is hereby granted, free of charge, to any person obtaining a copy of this software and associated documentation files (the "Software"), to deal in the Software without restriction, including without limitation the rights to use, copy, modify, merge, publish, distribute, sublicense, and/or sell copies of the Software, and to permit persons to whom the Software is furnished to do so, subject to the following conditions:

The above copyright notice and this permission notice shall be included in all copies or substantial portions of the Software.

THE SOFTWARE IS PROVIDED "AS IS", WITHOUT WARRANTY OF ANY KIND, EXPRESS OR IMPLIED, INCLUDING BUT NOT LIMITED TO THE WARRANTIES OF MERCHANTABILITY, FITNESS FOR A PARTICULAR PURPOSE AND NONINFRINGEMENT. IN NO EVENT SHALL THE AUTHORS OR COPYRIGHT HOLDERS BE LIABLE FOR ANY CLAIM, DAMAGES OR OTHER LIABILITY, WHETHER IN AN ACTION OF CONTRACT, TORT OR OTHERWISE, ARISING FROM, OUT OF OR IN CONNECTION WITH THE SOFTWARE OR THE USE OR OTHER DEALINGS IN THE SOFTWARE.

8.6.4. Lua License

Lua is covered by the MIT License similar to NodeMCU. The license text can be downloaded from http://www.lua.org/license.html.

8.6.5. ESPlorer License

ESPlorer is coveres by by GNU general Public License (GPL) V2. The license text can be downloaded from http://www.gnu.org/licenses/gpl-2.0.html

9. Index

10. Important Links

Inside the text many links were placed to point to datasheets, references, tutorials and further information.

Here are some links I see important as entry points for experimenting with NodeMCU on ESP8266:

- NodeMCU Repository
  https://github.com/nodemcu

- NodeMCU BBS
  http://bbs.nodemcu.com/

- Sample programs at Sourceforge
  http://sourceforge.net/projects/nodemcu/

- Custom Firmware Builds
  http://frightanic.com/nodemcu-custom-build/

- NodeMCU Blog
  https://cknodemcu.wordpress.com/

11. Other titles of the author

Further information is available on the following websites:

www.ckuehnel.ch & www.ckskript.ch

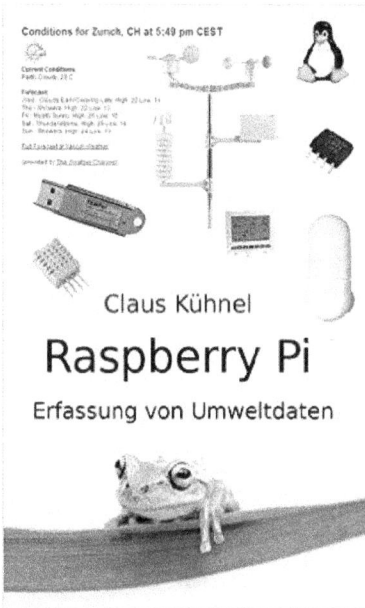

Conditions for Zurich, CH at 5:49 pm CEST

Claus Kühnel

Raspberry Pi

Erfassung von Umweltdaten

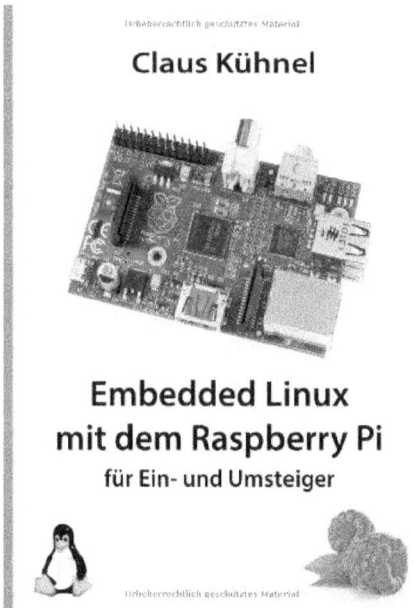

Claus Kühnel

Embedded Linux
mit dem Raspberry Pi
für Ein- und Umsteiger

ARDUINO

Arduino

Hard- und Software
Open Source Plattform

Claus Kühnel

Lua

Lua

Einsatz von Lua in
Embedded Systems

Claus Kühnel und Daniel Zwirner

2., bearbeitete und erweiterte Auflage

Notes

Your opinion or findings may also benefit others.

Here you will find space to record your notes, additions and proposals.

Please let us know your opinion on the book and use this opportunity in the interests of the entire readership.

The author's email address is info(at)ckskript.ch.